HOME CARE & UPKEEP

Created and designed
by the editorial staff
of ORTHO Books

Project Editor	Anne Coolman
Writers	B. Gay Ballard
	Tracy Craig
Designers	John Williams
	Barbara Ziller
Illustrator	Jon Larson
Photographer	Michael Lamotte
Photographic Stylist	Sara Slavin

Ortho Books

Publisher
Robert L. Iacopi

Editorial Director
Min S. Yee

Managing Editor
Anne Coolman

Horticultural Editor
Michael D. Smith

Senior Editor
Kenneth R. Burke

Production Manager
Laurie Sheldon

Editors
Barbara J. Ferguson
Sally W. Smith

Horticulturists
Michael D. McKinley
Deni W. Stein

Production Assistant
Darcie S. Furlan

Editorial Assistants
Laurie A. Black
Anne D. Pederson
William F. Yusavage

National Sales Manager
Garry P. Wellman

Operations/Distribution
William T. Pletcher

Operations Assistant
Donna M. White

Administrative Assistant
Georgiann Wright

Address all inquiries to:
Ortho Books
Chevron Chemical Company
Consumer Products Division
575 Market Street
San Francisco, CA 94105

ISBN 0-89721-014-X

Library of Congress Catalog Card
Number 82-63129

Chevron Chemical Company
575 Market Street, San Francisco, CA 94105

Acknowledgments

Technical Consultants

Gary Bowens
Professional Carpet Drycleaning
Concord, CA

Pat Brook
Contractor
Pleasant Hill, CA

Fred Brunswig
Electrical Contractor
Lafayette, CA

Larry Carter
Mortensen's Carpets
Oakland, CA

John Charlot
Landscape Contractor
Alamo, CA

Neil Crockett
Pianos
Walnut Creek, CA

Ron Duce
Contractor
Walnut Creek, CA

Jim Gallagher
Contra Costa Appliance
Walnut Creek, CA

Chief Inspector Darrell Harguth
Contra Costa County
Consolidated Fire District
Pleasant Hill, CA

Trish Hawkins
Upholsterer
Walnut Creek, CA

Theo Kahle
Capricornus
Berkeley, CA

Brent Kone
Pacific Ceiling Systems
Pacheco, CA

Don Meyers
Orlando Utilities Commission
Orlando, FL

Robyn Moulding
Colorways Fabrics
Concord, CA

John Power
City of Chicago
Building Inspector's Office
Chicago, IL

Art Slater
Senior Environmental Health and
   Safety Technologist
UC Berkeley
Berkeley, CA

Thomas W. Smith
American Building Maintenance Company
San Francisco, CA

Research Assistants

Nancy Burgess
Sidney Davenport
Bonnie McClean
Janet Powell
Judith Wood
Ami Zwicker

Copyediting

Editcetera
Berkeley, CA

Typesetting

Vera Allen
Castro Valley, CA

Color Separation

Colorscan
Mountain View, CA

Special Thanks to:

Catherine Black
Karen Bodman
Kathleen Carroll
Selma Hassen
Duane and Ghida Heaps
Sharon Parker
Steve Sardella
Victor Seckler
Sandra Whelpley
Paul Vincent Wiseman
   Interior Design
   San Francisco, CA

Front Cover

Whatever the surface or item in your
home, caring for it is easier when you
know which cleaning agents and
techniques to use. Clockwise from top
left: wood floors, page 23; tile walls,
page 30; pots and pans, page 58;
upholstery, page 36; silver (and other
metals), page 61; coffee and other
stains, pages 38–51; wicker furniture,
page 35; leather, page 56; (center)
cleaning tools and equipment, pages
8–9.

Back Cover

For helpful guidelines in selecting and
storing tools, equipment, and household supplies, see pages 8–15.

Page 1

Writers Gay Ballard (left) and Tracy
Craig (right)

HOME CARE & UPKEEP

HOME CARE BASICS

Use this chapter to help
organize your storage and
cleaning systems, choose
wisely from a vast array
of household products,
prevent accidents, and
protect your property.

Creating a beautiful environment can be wonderfully satisfying. Experimenting with colors and textures, arranging furniture and treasured possessions, and refining the look and feel of a room, are all channels for personal expression. And the care and attention you put into your home is often returned to you when the environment you create lifts and nurtures your spirit and provides a source of rejuvenation and refreshment for you, your family, and guests.

No matter how lavishly or simply you design your environment, one key to a beautiful home is knowledge—knowing how to care for all its surfaces and contents, and knowing how to create and maintain a sense of order and cleanliness. With this knowledge, home care is easier and less time consuming.

Few people have the time, energy, or inclination to make home care a full-time occupation, but basic time-management techniques can help you keep a general sense of order, even on especially busy days. Simple five-minute jobs (organizing a drawer, cleaning under the sink, collecting and organizing small tools, and so on) will help you keep up with home-care tasks, and help you feel good about your home's condition. For more ideas on saving time, see pages 6 and 7.

Getting others involved in the care of your home is one way to tackle big jobs. It can make those overwhelming tasks more enjoyable since it's much more fun to clean, organize, and even redecorate or remodel when your family and friends help out. Some people swap cleaning time at each other's houses, or get together on a weekend to get a large job done quickly. This kind of exchange can make a task such as painting a room a social event rather than an isolated chore.

When you need special help, consider using professionals. There are pros for almost every home-related task—for example, full-time, part-time, and one-time housecleaners, and specialists such as carpet- and up-holstery-cleaning services. They charge by the hour or by the job and may work in teams to get the job done fast. By watching them work, you may be able to do the same job yourself the next time around. Home-care consultants can help you get your storage and closets in shape and often have color and design experience as well, so they can give you decorating ideas or work with you to organize your wardrobe.

Whenever you hire anyone to come into your home, whether it's a housecleaning service, repairman, or pest-control operator, make sure the person is bonded and insured. Professional electrical, plumbing, building, and pest-control services should be licensed, as well. Before the work starts, make sure you both agree about what they will do, what their charges will be, and when the job will start and end (especially if you are hiring an independent person or service). If you have a question about a specific service or a problem with their work, your local Better Business Bureau can help.

Whatever your style and system of home care and upkeep, use this book as a reference manual for all your routine and periodic tasks, as well as for special problems. The rest of this chapter tells you more about getting organized, and about which tools and products are available to make home care easier and more efficient. You will also find some important home-safety and security guidelines, including a basic first-aid kit for medical emergencies, and methods for securing your home against burglars. The second chapter, "Your Home's Interior" (pages 19–71), shows how to care for the inside of your home and its contents. It includes a number of handy reference charts for such tasks as fabric care and stain removal. The third chapter, "Your Home's Systems and Exterior" (pages 73–91), details periodic maintenance checks you can make to help prevent major repairs.

Throughout the book you will find references to other Ortho books—specifically, *Basic Home Repairs, Basic Wiring, Basic Plumbing,* and *Energy-Saving Projects for the Home.* Additional Ortho books that will help you keep your home in its best condition are *How to Design & Build Storage Projects, Basic Remodeling Techniques,* and *Basic Carpentry Techniques.*

Masonry floor, oriental rug, painted wood trim, wallpaper, wood cabinetry, stainless steel, glass, ceramics, plastic laminate: Even in a corner of one room, there may be a dozen different surfaces to care for. This book contains the information you need to make cleaning tasks fast and easy.

ORGANIZING & CLEANING

Why be organized? There are many possible answers to this question, but one is that being organized eases the flow of daily life; it limits unnecessary obstacles to the flow of routine activities. No matter what "system" of organization you use or what that system may look like to others, caring for your home and its contents will be easier and less time-consuming if *you* feel organized.

Improving your level of organization does not necessarily mean restructuring your whole life. Whether or not you feel comfortable with your current approach to household order, the tips on these two pages are designed to simplify your home care tasks and to make your life easier. If you're looking for a way to overhaul your entire organization system, start with Ortho's book, *How to Design & Build Storage Projects,* and then look at the wide variety of other books devoted to time- and home-management systems. There is no single perfect system. Just find the approach that works best for you.

Household clutter and storage

No matter what else you do, keep clutter under control. Wherever it is—at your desk, in your garage, or on the bottom of a closet—deal with the clutter first. When you sift through the articles in these areas, ask yourself if you really need them. If you tell yourself, "I think I'll keep this—I may need it someday," chances are you won't. Except in cases of cosmic conflict, throw such questionable clutter into the garbage, give it away, or sell it. If the articles are seasonal, store them out of sight.

The paper glut

After getting rid of household clutter, develop a system for organizing the carloads of paper you shuffle around daily. It doesn't matter what the system is as long as it makes sense to you. There are certain papers you need to keep for legal or insurance purposes. The two lists that follow itemize those papers you should keep in your desk (or in a place where they can be retrieved), and those papers and documents you should keep in your safety deposit box.

What papers to keep at home

□ Bank statements and canceled checks (keep 3 to 5 years)
□ Current bills payable
□ Instruction manuals and hang-tags
□ Insurance policies (keep originals at home; keep a *list* of policies in safety deposit box)
□ Inventory and appraisals of personal property (keep copies at home; keep originals in safety deposit box)
□ Invoices paid (keep 3 to 5 years)
□ Medical and dental records (keep them up to date)
□ Real property improvement records (canceled checks, photos)
□ Sales slips (sales taxes are tax deductible in some states)
□ Service and repair records
□ Social Security cards (carry original with you; keep copy in safety deposit box)
□ Tax records (keep returns and records at home; keep canceled checks of tax payments in safety deposit box; keep all records 6 to 10 years)
□ Warranties and serial numbers (appliances, electronic equipment, tools)

What papers to keep in a safety deposit box

□ Auto ownership papers
□ Bank savings and deposit records
□ Contracts, deeds, leases, loan agreements, mortgages, promissory notes, trust deeds
□ Credit card numbers
□ Family documents (adoption, birth, death, divorce, marriage)
□ Insurance policies (keep a *list* of policies in safety deposit box; keep originals at home)
□ Inventory and appraisals of personal property (keep originals in safety deposit box; keep copies at home)
□ Military records
□ Naturalization papers
□ Patent papers
□ Pension papers
□ Powers of attorney
□ Savings and deposit records
□ Social Security cards (keep copy in safety deposit box; carry original with you)
□ Stocks and bonds
□ Tax records (keep canceled checks of tax payments in safety deposit box; keep other records at home)
□ Wills

When the papers you need are organized in some sort of filing system, go through every other piece of paper you have in drawers, on shelves, or in piles on your desk. Throw out everything you don't want or need. The more ruthless you are in this process, the better your chances of uncluttering your life. Again, the point of this periodic exercise is simply to unclog the system—to keep your house and mind from being filled with unnecessary "stuff." Then create places to put those papers you really want to keep. (See item 4 in the next section.)

Routine and periodic cleaning

There are two basic philosophies of cleaning: One is to go about your activities with the idea that cleaning comes *later*—whether "later" is in an hour or on Saturday, the idea is that you'll eventually clean up the mess; meanwhile it's okay to let the messes accumulate because it's not "cleaning time." The second approach is to go about your activities with the idea of maintaining the level of order and cleanliness you're comfortable with—you clean up as you go. It is simply a subtle twist in approach. Either approach works, but the advantage of the second is that your home is generally more comfortable because it is rarely a total disaster, and when you do have a couple of hours for more intensive cleaning, the routine jobs are out of the way.

The list below notes some of the basics of this approach:

1. Pick up clutter when you see it—don't just step over it again and again.

2. Even if you don't intend to wash the dishes right

after a meal, put them in a sinkful of water to soak, or in the dishwasher.

3. Wipe up spills as soon as they happen, and soak stained clothing in water until you can treat a stain.

4. Handle pieces of paper only once. Designate a drawer or shelf to hold the variety of papers that come into your home. Look through everything as soon as it arrives and sort it into piles: newspapers and magazines (and junk mail, if you read it) in a "read later" pile; bills in a second; and correspondence in a third. Periodically sort through the "read later" pile and toss out the items you know you'll never get to. When you're through paying bills or responding to letters, file your copies of invoices paid, and throw out or file old letters.

5. Keep your cleaning supplies organized (see pages 8–9).

6. When you have something you need to deliver—a pile of clothes to take to the dry cleaners, library books to return—put it in the car as soon as the thought occurs to you. Don't let these piles clutter up your house.

7. When messes build up and you're faced with an overwhelming cleaning job (and you don't have the time or energy for a five-hour cleaning binge), use a basic time-management technique: break down the overwhelming job into small segments. Whenever you have five minutes, don't think you can't do the big job just because you only have five minutes—instead, work on one of the segments. If you need to clean out the garage, for example, take five minutes on Tuesday just to pick up miscellaneous pieces of junk and throw them out. Take another five minutes on Wednesday to put all the long-handled garden tools in one place. As you pick away at an overwhelming job, you'll find that you don't really need five uninterrupted hours after all. You may need only an hour or less on Saturday to finish up.

8. Encourage other household members to join the "clean-as-you-go" effort.

Cleaning traditions

Cleaning techniques and systems are "traditions" that are handed down from one generation to the next. Some families teach children many cleaning and repair skills. Other families may teach children nothing more than how to put clothes in a laundry basket. Consequently, there is no standardized body of knowledge about home care to which every growing child has access. Whatever your own level of knowledge or skill may be, this book serves as a reference for questions related to this body of knowledge. On the next two pages, you'll find information on home care tools and equipment; on pages 10–15, information on household products; and on pages 16–17, guidelines for home safety and security.

A clean, well-organized desk is a major key to household order. Your entire house tends to feel less cluttered when your desk is not covered with piles of bills and junk mail.

TOOLS & EQUIPMENT

Home care is much easier with top-quality, durable tools and equipment. There may be nothing more frustrating than trying to accomplish simple tasks with ineffective tools—everything becomes unnecessarily difficult, time-consuming, and annoying. If you have many square feet of wood flooring to clean and wax, you'll save years of aggravation by purchasing a buffing machine instead of renting a buffer every time you wax, or trying to get by with rags or a dust mop. And if you purchase the best buffer you can find, you'll be happier with the results and avoid frequent repairs. So, when investing in home care tools and equipment, make sure you get all the tools you need and shop around for quality. The effort will ultimately save you time and money.

Because home care tasks are a daily part of life, it makes sense to make tools and supplies as accessible as possible. If you can't find the dustpan or screwdriver, or if it is three rooms away when you need it, the job you need it for will take much longer than necessary. The most common approach is to store major pieces of equipment and replacement supplies in a central area and to store tools and supplies needed for specific jobs in the room where they will be used. Another approach is to create a portable cleaning cart—a variation on the supply carts used by commercial janitorial services—to hold all the equipment and cleaning products you use for floors, furniture, and fixtures throughout the house. A small stain-removing kit and some basic repair tools can be included on the cart or kept in the central storage area. Wheeling a cart around is simpler than carrying a multitude of items from room to room and may make cleaning easier, particularly in a large house.

The photographs on these two pages identify a range of tools that will help you accomplish most routine and periodic tasks, make minor repairs, and cope with plumbing and electrical emergencies. Reading this section in conjunction with "Household Products" on pages 10–15 will give you a good idea of what tools and products will help you keep your home at its best with the least time and effort.

Tools

The following list will give you an idea of the basic tools and equipment to keep on hand for cleaning and making minor repairs.

☐ **Lamb's wool duster and extension handle**
(Extension handle makes dusting walls and ceilings easy.)

☐ **Upright vacuum**
☐ **Canister vacuum with a beater brush carpet attachment**
☐ **Wet-dry vacuum**
(You may wish to have two vacuum cleaners: one for floors and one for stairs and upholstery. Vacuums for carpets should have a beater brush. Some canister vacuums have a beater brush carpet attachment. Wet-dry vacuums may be a good alternative, particularly if your home has a lot of resilient floor coverings.)

☐ **Sponge, rag, or string floor mops**
(Get two: one for scrubbing and one for applying polishes.)
☐ **Dust mop**
(Use unoiled mops on waxed floors.)
☐ **Broom**
☐ **Push broom**
☐ **Dustpans**
(Dustpans are also great for scooping up fireplace ashes, leaves, and old floor wax.)
☐ **Buffing machine**
(Good for scrubbing floors, applying wax, and buffing waxed floors)

☐ **Synthetic sponges**
☐ **Dry sponge**
(A chemically treated sponge good for cleaning nonwashable walls and ceilings)

☐ **Soft scrubbing pads**
(Good for surfaces susceptible to scratching)
☐ **Miscellaneous absorbent cleaning cloths**
(Use terry cloth for cleaning walls and ceilings, and cleaning and brushing up the nap on upholstered furniture.)
☐ **Drop cloths**
☐ **Rubber gloves**

☐ **Artist's brushes**
(Good for applying glue to small surfaces)
☐ **Upholstery brush**
☐ **Grout brush**
(Good for scrubbing masonry and tile grout)
☐ **Wire brush**
(Good for scrubbing difficult stains from masonry and stone, and for removing creosote from chimneys and stovepipes)
☐ **Bottle brush**
☐ **Refrigerator coil brush**
☐ **Radiator brush**

☐ **Floor squeegee**
(Good for scraping up old floor wax)
☐ **Window squeegee**

☐ **Screwdrivers**
☐ **Utility knife and blades**
☐ **Adjustable wrench**
☐ **Slip-joint pliers**
☐ **Putty knives**
☐ **Curved-claw hammer**
☐ **White glue**
☐ **Yellow wood glue**
☐ **Sandpaper**
☐ **C-clamps**
☐ **Emery paper**
☐ **Steel wool**
(Good for scrubbing difficult stains on wood, metal, and plastic surfaces)
☐ **Monkey wrench**
☐ **Plunger**
☐ **Flashlight**
☐ **Continuity tester**
(Use to test fuses and batteries.)
☐ **Voltage tester**
(Use to test outlets and grounding.)
☐ **Electrical tape**

Left: In addition to the standard cleaning tools and equipment, some tools for specific tasks are shown here: dry sponges for cleaning non-washable walls, a refrigerator coil brush, a wire brush for cleaning brick and chimney flues, and a grout brush for cleaning tile walls and floors.
Right: The most basic "quick-repair" kit should include a voltage tester to test electrical outlets, and clamps to hold glued surfaces.

HOUSEHOLD PRODUCTS

The number of products available for cleaning and caring for your home and belongings can seem staggering. This book itself refers to over 180 household products. They range from common items found in your kitchen, such as vinegar and baking soda, to products designed for very specific purposes, such as fiberglass cleaners and stove blacking.

There are household products for cleaning, protecting, deodorizing, patching and repairing, controlling pests, lubricating, and removing spots and stains. Because a wide variety of care situations will arise in any home, a variety of specific products will be called for. However, this doesn't mean you should stock your home with every conceivable cleaning or protective agent you can find. In most cases your usual supply of products will be quite sufficient. But when you face special problems—such as stains that need removing, or special surfaces that need cleaning—you may want to investigate products you have not used before.

The next few pages contain an alphabetical list of household products and agents in various forms: those that are used in their "raw" form (ammonia, alcohol, and so on); those that may require special precautions (bleaches, oven cleaners, drain cleaners, and so forth); those that can be used for a wide variety of purposes (vinegar, baking soda); and those that may simply be unfamiliar to you (fuller's earth, powdered graphite). Products designed for specific purposes are described within the text of this book—floor-care products, upholstery cleaners, and so on.

Finally, there is a short glossary, which serves as a reference for terms with which you may be unfamiliar. Household products are often categorized by the nature of their properties. Abrasives, for example, are "scrubbers." Scouring powders are considered abrasives. If you have any questions about the products mentioned in this book, just flip back to this section.

Acetone

Acetone is used to dissolve and remove difficult stains from.hard surfaces such as porcelain, and from fabrics. Nail polish remover, available at grocery stores, contains enough acetone to use on light stains that respond to this agent. The Stain chart, pages 42–51, sometimes recommends acetone or amyl acetate. Of these two agents, amyl acetate is the less likely to damage fabrics, so you may wish to try it first. Do not use acetone on acetates, dacron, elastics, felt, fur, leather, metallics, polyester, rayon, rubber, silk, triacetates, or wool. When removing stains from these fabrics, repeat the other steps noted in the chart. Acetone is moderately toxic and extremely flammable. Avoid contact with skin and eyes. Keep away from children. Avoid breathing vapor.

Alcohol

In this book, alcohol refers to ethyl alcohol, a mildly disinfecting, rapidly evaporating solvent often called rubbing or grain alcohol. "Denatured alcohol" is ethyl alcohol with one or more toxic substances added to prevent its use as a beverage. Use ethyl alcohol to clean and remove mildew from hard surfaces, candles, tools, leather, carpets, mattresses, and upholstery. *To remove stains:* Before using alcohol on any fabric, test on an inconspicuous spot to make certain dyes will not be affected. Ethyl alcohol is slightly toxic. Denatured alcohol may be poisonous, especially if it contains methyl alcohol (wood alcohol).

All-purpose cleaners

Liquid all-purpose cleaners are mostly water with detergents and other additives, such as ammonia, disinfectants, or solvents. Dilute according to package instructions, and use to clean hard surfaces, floors, and most plastics. (*Note:* they may dissolve flat wall paint.) Do not use on carpets, rugs, or upholstery—they may leave a dirt-attracting film. Use full strength to remove wax and dissolve paint. Leave all-purpose cleaning solutions on the surface long enough to let the chemicals work—don't scrub immediately—and always rinse thoroughly.

Powdered all-purpose cleaners can be used, dry, as a substitute for scouring powders. (An effective substitute all-purpose cleaning solution is ¼ c ammonia and 3 tbsp washing soda dissolved in ½ gal water.) May be toxic—read label for cautions. Keep all cleaners, especially the pleasantly scented liquids, out of reach of children.

Ammonia

Ammonia is an alkaline cleaner and a mild bleach. Vary the strength of the solution to fit the job, as indicated throughout this book. Use with caution on finished or painted surfaces—the ammonia may dissolve the finish. *To remove stains:* Do not use on acetate, dacron, triacetate, or wool; instead, use vinegar. Test on an inconspicuous spot before using. Sometimes a combination of ammonia and hydrogen peroxide is recommended in the Stain chart on pages 42–51. This mixture produces a bleaching action, and can be used when other bleaches are too strong for the fabric. See Hydrogen peroxide for the cautions that accompany this combination. Vinegar cannot be substituted for ammonia in this case. Never mix ammonia with other household cleaners or with products containing chlorine—the combination produces toxic vapors. Ammonia is poisonous. Keep all forms, especially the pleasantly scented liquids, out of reach of children. Avoid contact with skin and eyes—may cause severe irritation. Avoid breathing vapor.

Amyl Acetate

A colorless liquid solvent, available from pharmacies in the form of banana oil, amyl acetate is used to remove stains from fabrics. The Stain chart, pages 42–51, sometimes recommends acetone or amyl acetate. Of these two chemicals, amyl acetate is the less likely to damage fabric, so you may wish to try it first. Do not use amyl acetate on acetates, dacron, elastics, felt, fur, leather, metallics, polyester, rayon, rubber, silk, triacetate, or wool. When removing stains from these fabrics, repeat other steps noted in the chart. Amyl acetate is moderately toxic and combustible. Avoid contact with skin and eyes. Avoid breathing vapor.

Baking soda

Common household baking soda is a non-toxic, versatile alkaline cleaner and absorbent. Some of its many uses are listed here:

□ Putting out oil and grease fires. Keep a box next to your stove.

□ Absorbing odors in your refrigerator. Keep an open box or bowl on a shelf.

□ Cleaning and deodorizing drains. Pour a handful down drains once a week, then follow with hot water.

□ Softening and deodorizing your laundry. Add ½ c to the rinse cycle.

□ Cleaning burned-on food from pots, pans, and ovens. Use a paste of baking soda and water.

□ Removing stains and odors from porcelain, ceramics, enamelware, coffee pots, plastic food containers, and thermos bottles. Use a paste of baking soda and water.

□ As a substitute scouring powder on most hard surfaces. Use dry—it will not scratch.

□ Shining silver, chromium, and glass. Use a solution of baking soda and water.

□ Removing stains from carpets and rugs. Use as an absorbent for wet stains. Sprinkle baking soda on the stain, leave it overnight, then vacuum it up. If some of the stain remains, follow instructions on the Stain chart, pages 42–51.

Bar soap

You can use common household bar soap to remove some grease stains from washable fabrics by rubbing and rinsing repeatedly. See page 46 for other ways to remove grease stains.

Bleaches

Bleaches are substances that remove color. From weakest to strongest, bleaches mentioned in this book are: lemon juice, ammonia and hydrogen peroxide, oxygen bleach, chlorine bleach, oxalic acid, and muriatic acid. Chlorine and oxygen bleaches are the two main types used for laundry and general household cleaning. Avoid all bleaches on chamois, chiffon, leather, rubber, and silk. The others, each listed separately on these pages, are used to remove stains.

Chlorine bleach. This comes in both liquid and powder forms. Most clothing labels indicate whether it is safe to use on the fabric. If there is no label, check the Fabric Care chart on pages 38–41, and test on an inconspicuous spot before using. Do not use chlorine bleach on acetate, linen, rayon, silk, spandex, or wool. Do not mix chlorine in metal containers—the metal speeds up the bleaching action and may stain the fabric. Never mix chlorine bleach with other household cleaners, especially those containing ammonia. The combination produces toxic vapors. Chlorine bleach is toxic. Keep out of reach of children. Avoid contact with skin and eyes. Avoid breathing vapor.

Oxygen (or peroxygen) bleaches. These generally come in powder form and can be used on almost all fabrics. Because the powders are highly alkaline, they can be

Periodically, wipe food preparation surfaces with a mild chlorine bleach solution to discourage bacteria. Rinse thoroughly and wipe dry.

extremely irritating to skin and eyes. Keep out of reach of children. Do not mix with other cleaning agents. Follow the package directions for the correct amounts in your laundry.

Bleaching stains: Sometimes stain removal is a two-step process—1) removing the staining material itself, and 2) bleaching out the color of that staining material. When bleach is recommended in the Stain chart, pages 42–51, use these guidelines for selecting the appropriate bleaching product:

□ Use lemon juice to lighten ivory.

□ Use hydrogen peroxide with a few drops ammonia added to bleach stains on fabrics that may be damaged by chlorine or oxygen bleaches. This combination is used as an alternative to other bleaches on non-washable fabrics, upholstery, carpets, and rugs; however, it can be used on most washable fabrics.

□ Use oxygen bleach for removing stains and dinginess from acrylic, permanent press, polyester, rayon, saran, spandex, and triacetate. Test before using on other fabrics.

□ Use chlorine bleach for removing stains and dinginess from white cotton fabric. In general, add 1 c to the wash cycle along with your detergent, or soak in a solution of ½ c per gal of water for up to half an hour before washing. (Chlorine bleach is also used to kill bacteria and to discourage mold and mildew on household surfaces.)

□ Use oxalic acid to bleach stains from masonry floors. Poisonous and highly irritating to skin, eyes, and mucous membranes.

□ Use muriatic acid to remove stains and efflorescence from brick and concrete. Poisonous and highly irritating to skin, eyes, and mucous membranes.

Cornmeal

Used as an absorbent to remove liquids and odors from fur rugs and clothing, and as a medium in which to store silver jewelry to keep it from tarnishing.

Cream of tartar

Available at grocery stores, cream of tartar is used in baking powders, and also alone as a leavening agent. Around the house, it is used to bleach stains from fabrics and metals. Toxic in large quantities if swallowed.

Detergents

The word *detergent* generally refers to a synthetic cleaner that will work in both hot and cold water. Laundry soap flakes, on the other hand, are made from natural animal or vegetable fats and do not work well in cold water. Soaps are more likely to leave a film than detergent and require an acid rinse—generally vinegar—to remove it. Cold-water soaps are actually mild detergents that readily dissolve in cold water. Laundry detergents often combine synthetic detergents, moisturizers, and other cleaning aids such as bleach, water conditioners, and agents that separate and dissolve dirt and grease. They can generally be used on any washable fabric except silk and wool—these fabrics require gentler detergent or soap. Some laundry detergents contain phosphates to soften hard water. Because phosphates are banned in some states for environmental reasons, you can boost the effectiveness of non-phosphate detergents by using water softeners such as washing soda. *To remove stains:* Liquid detergent, used in combination with vinegar or ammonia, is a common stain-removing agent. Follow directions in the Stain chart on pages 42–51. A few detergents are toxic and caustic. Read labels for cautions. Avoid prolonged contact with skin and eyes.

Disinfectants

Liquid disinfectants kill household bacteria, mold, and mildew. Some all-purpose cleaners contain disinfectants—some disinfectant liquids contain all-purpose cleaners. Use to prevent and kill mold and mildew, and to deodorize and sanitize hard surfaces such as bathroom floors and fixtures. Some disinfectants are toxic—read labels for cautions.

Drain cleaners

Drain cleaners and oven cleaners containing lye are the most dangerous cleaners in your house, and must, therefore, be used with caution. Do not use on aluminum, rubber, plastic, electrical parts, or porcelain. Follow label instructions carefully. As a substitute for drain cleaners, try washing soda and a plunger. To prevent clogged drains, pour baking soda, washing soda, vinegar, ammonia, or boiling water down the drains once a week. Use drain strainers to catch hair and food, and dispose of grease and oils in containers instead of down the drain. Drain cleaners are caustic and poisonous. Avoid contact with skin and eyes. Carefully store out of reach of children (preferably in a locked cabinet).

Dry-cleaning fluids

Liquid dry-cleaning fluids are solvents that lift and dissolve grease and dirt. They are used to remove stains—especially grease stains—from fabrics. They are especially useful on one-sided fabrics such as rugs, carpets, and upholstery because they evaporate quickly. Do not use on plastic, rubber, or suede. If removing a grease stain on leather, wipe dry-cleaning fluid off quickly to avoid damage. Dry-cleaning fluids may be flammable. All are poisonous. Read label for cautions. Avoid contact with skin and eyes. Avoid breathing vapors, and provide adequate ventilation when using. Keep away from children, preferably in a locked cabinet. If you have any dry-cleaning solutions containing carbon tetrachloride, be advised that this chemical has been banned from commercial products since 1971 by the Consumer Product Safety Commission. Call your local health department for disposal instructions.

Enzyme products

Enzyme laundry products dissolve or "eat" organic matter. They are designed to remove protein stains such as egg from fabrics. They may come in powder form with a small amount of detergent added, or they may be added to other laundry detergents. Some states have banned enzyme laundry products for environmental reasons. If you live in such a state, use washing soda instead. *To remove stains:* Use an enzyme product rather than a laundry detergent with enzymes added. Do not use enzymes on linen, wool, or silk—they will dissolve the fabric as well as the stain. Read package directions and cautions carefully. May cause allergic reaction. Avoid contact with eyes. Avoid prolonged contact with skin.

Fabric softeners

These liquids or liquid-impregnated sheets are moisturizers that swell the fabric with moisture, making it feel softer and repelling static electricity. The moisture remains in the fabric through several washings, so you don't have to add them each time you wash or dry. Some people have an allergic reaction to the chemicals and perfumes used, developing a skin rash or asthma. If this occurs, discontinue use. Follow package instructions.

Fuller's earth

A fine powder used to absorb oil, grease, and odors from non-washable surfaces. When combined with dry-cleaning fluid, it is also used to clean non-washable wall coverings. Available at paint stores and home improvement centers.

Glycerine

Used commercially in cosmetics and glues to hold moisture. In the house, glycerine is used alone to soften old stains before they are removed or is mixed with other stain-removing agents. Available from pharmacies.

Hydrogen peroxide

Hydrogen peroxide is used as a mild disinfectant and bleach. *To remove stains:* Hydrogen peroxide may be recommended in the Stain chart, pages 42–51, as a stain removing agent in combination with ammonia. Use when chlorine or oxygen bleaches are too strong for the fabric. This mixture produces an irritating vapor, and should never be stored. Hydrogen peroxide is non-toxic in a 3% solution, but toxic when combined with ammonia. Avoid breathing fumes, especially when combined with ammonia. Avoid contact with eyes.

Linseed oil

A lubricating polish available in both boiled and raw forms. Never try to boil raw linseed oil—it may ignite. Danish oils are often boiled linseed oil with a dark stain added. Lemon oils may be boiled linseed oil with lemon oil added. Pure linseed oil is digestible, but boiled linseed oil is toxic, and should not be taken internally because other chemicals are added. Keep pleasantly scented oils out of reach of children.

Lye

A strong alkali that dissolves grease, paint, and varnish. It is used commercially in cleaning agents, detergents, paint removers, and oven and drain cleaners. It is also used to remove brown scales from pewter. Lye is poisonous and caustic. Avoid contact with skin and eyes. Keep away from children, preferably in a locked cabinet. Avoid breathing fumes. Provide adequate ventilation when using. Always read label for cautions.

Metal cleaners

All-purpose metal cleaners are available, but they are generally too abrasive for silver, stainless steel, and chromium. For more information on metals in general, see Metals, page 61. Some are toxic and caustic—read labels for cautions.

Mildewcides

Commercial mildewcides often come in pump spray form and are generally chlorine based. There are also mildew preventives that contain fungicides. These come in block form and can be hung in damp areas to discourage mold and mildew from growing. Follow label directions on both products. Fabrics damaged by chlorine will be damaged by chlorine-based mildewcides. Both forms of mildewcides may be toxic. Read label for cautions. Avoid contact with skin and eyes. Keep out of reach of children. Avoid breathing fumes.

Mineral oil

Mineral oil is used to protect metal surfaces and tools from tarnish. It is also commonly used in combination

Prevent the growth of mildew in bathrooms by replacing conventional light fixtures with heating spotlights, and by improving the flow of air with fans or open windows.

with dry-cleaning fluid to keep it from evaporating too rapidly, and to soften stains.

Moth repellants

These are odorous blocks or crystals that repel and kill moths and other insects. Very little goes a long way. All are poisonous, and some are flammable. Avoid contact with skin and eyes. Avoid breathing fumes. Keep away from children.

HOUSEHOLD PRODUCTS

Muriatic acid

This is hydrochloric acid used to remove stains from brick and concrete. It will corrode metal, rubber, and plastic. Muriatic acid is poisonous and caustic. Avoid contact with skin and eyes. Do not mix with other cleaners—the combination may produce toxic fumes. Keep away from children, preferably in a locked cabinet.

Neat's-foot oil

A lubricant for leather and parchment. Available from shoe repair shops.

Oxalic acid

Oxalic acid is a bleach used commercially in metal, floor, and furniture polishes, and paint, rust, and stain removers. Available at hardware stores as a stain remover for masonry and wood floors. Oxalic acid is poisonous and caustic. Avoid contact with skin and eyes. Avoid breathing vapors. Do not mix with other cleaners. Keep away from children.

Pre-wash products

There are a number of pre-wash sprays available. All of them are similar, and some liquid laundry detergents serve the same purpose. Usually the label suggests that you spray or pour the product on the spot or stain, let it sit for 5 to 15 minutes, and then wash as usual. When a pre-wash product is recommended in the Stain chart, pages 42–51, for non-washable fabrics, carpets, rugs, and upholstery, it is preferable to use a pre-wash spray. Spray the spot once only—it is a detergent, and will take some time to sponge out. Most pre-wash products are non-toxic.

Pumice powder

A medium abrasive used to polish hard surfaces such as marble. Available at home improvement centers.

Rottenstone powder

A soft abrasive that is mixed with oils and used to clean soft metals. Available at paint stores.

Rust preventives

These products are used in paints and as an oil, which seals surfaces from the air and thereby prevents rust. Rust preventives are poisonous and flammable. Avoid contact with skin and eyes. Avoid breathing vapor. Keep away from children, preferably in a locked cabinet. Available at hardware stores and home-improvement centers.

Rust removers

Rust removers dissolve rust. They are poisonous and caustic. Keep away from children, preferably in a locked cabinet. Avoid contact with skin and eyes. Avoid breathing vapor. Available at hardware stores and home-improvement centers. There are also rust removers for fabrics, available at some fabric stores.

Scouring powders

These are abrasive powders mixed with detergents, and sometimes with bleach. As an alternative to scouring powders, you can use dry dishwasher soap, baking soda, or TSP and soft scouring pads, which will avoid scratching surfaces. Scouring powders containing bleach are toxic. Do not mix with other cleaners, especially those containing ammonia—the combination may produce highly irritating vapor.

Soap flakes

Laundry soap flakes are used for delicate fabrics such as lingerie and baby clothes. The flakes must be completely dissolved in water and rinsed thoroughly, or else they will leave a dirt-attracting, stiff film. To remove the residue, add 1 c vinegar to the rinse cycle. Soap produces suds that can clog your washing machine and sewer; follow package instructions for the correct amounts to use. If you are sensitive to detergents, you will find soap less irritating. Non-toxic.

Stain-removing agents

Most stains can be dealt with by using common household products such as liquid detergent, ammonia, vinegar, alcohol, baking soda, prewash and enzyme laundry products, and so on. A few products, recommended in the Stain chart on pages 42–51, may not be staples among your cleaning supplies: dry-cleaning fluid, acetone, amyl acetate, glycerine, hydrogen peroxide, mineral oil, and washing soda. Of these, dry-cleaning fluid, mineral oil, hydrogen peroxide, and washing soda are handy to have around for taking quick action on many stains, particularly stains on non-washable fabrics. Remember that stain-removing agents affect the stain itself *and* the fabric or surface. The agent is recommended for its ability to work on the stain. Most of the cautions concern the fabric and safe use of the agent. Whenever you use one of these agents to remove a stain, check the individual agent in this chapter, and the Fabric Care chart on pages 38–41.

Toilet cleaners

Designed to be used either in the toilet bowl or in the tank, in-tank cleaners add chemicals each time the toilet is flushed. The in-tank types contain mostly detergent and dye. Those used to scrub the bowl are generally acid-based, and must be used with caution. Liquid chlorine bleach or an all-purpose cleaner are good substitutes for cleaning, deodorizing, and disinfecting. Bowl cleaners are corrosive poisons. Avoid contact with skin and eyes. Keep away from children, preferably in a locked cabinet. Do not mix toilet cleaners with other cleaners. Do not use on metal parts.

Trisodium phosphate (TSP)

A strong alkali cleaner for floors and walls. Always rinse repeatedly to remove any residue. TSP is caustic. Avoid contact with skin and eyes.

Vinegar

Vinegar, like baking soda, has many uses. It is non-toxic. Some of its uses are listed below.

☐ Absorbing odors. Place open bowls of vinegar in

smoke-filled rooms, and boil white vinegar to eliminate cooking odors.

  □ Cutting grease when washing dishes. Add a few drops to dishwashing solution.

  □ Cutting grease and soap residue in your laundry. Add 1 c to the final rinse.

  □ Cleaning and deodorizing drains. Pour 1 c down the drain, let sit for half an hour, then follow with hot water.

  □ Instead of commercial window-cleaning solutions. Add 1 tbsp to 1 pt spray bottle of water.

  □ Removing odors from inside refrigerators, lunch boxes, jars, and bottles. Use full strength.

  □ Removing stains. Use vinegar instead of ammonia when removing stains from fabrics damaged by ammonia, or combine vinegar with detergent and water. Follow instructions in the Stain chart, pages 42–51.

  □ Removing stains from china—especially tea and coffee stains—and burned-on food from pots and pans. Use full strength to soak china, pots, and pans.

Washing soda
A water conditioner used to soften water and boost detergent effectiveness. Also used as a cleaner by itself or mixed with water. *To remove stains:* Use as a substitute for enzyme products to soak or sponge stains on almost all fabrics. Washing soda is highly alkaline, therefore caustic. Avoid prolonged contact with skin and eyes.

Whiting
A soft abrasive (also called putty powder) used to remove scratches from metals and marble. Available from paint stores and home improvement centers.

GLOSSARY
Abrasives. Powders used to scrub or rub away, such as putty powder, rottenstone powder, pumice powder, whiting, salt, scouring powders, emery paper, and sandpaper. Routine use of abrasive scouring powders or pads on shiny surfaces (such as stainless steel) or porous surfaces (such as porcelain) will eventually wear down and scratch these surfaces, giving dirt and bacteria more places to hide. Instead, use non-abrasive powders such as TSP, baking soda, and dishwasher detergent.

Absorbents. Used to absorb moisture and liquids, absorbents include powders (such as baking soda), cornmeal, fuller's earth, bread crumbs, and salt.

Acids and alkalis. The chemical compounds in most cleaning solutions are either acidic or alkaline. One neutralizes the other. Much of cleaning and stain removing is simply a process of neutralization. Acids include vinegar, lemon juice, oxalic acid, and muriatic acid. Alkalis include ammonia, baking soda, lye, washing soda, and salt. If your alkaline cleaner leaves a film, neutralize it with an acid such as vinegar. Acids also have bleaching properties. The stronger alkalis, such as ammonia and lye, are potentially as caustic as the strong acids and should be handled with as much care.

Caustic or corrosive. Chemicals that destroy or burn tissue are called caustic or corrosive. Some alkaline cleaners (such as lye), and some acid cleaners (such as mu-

Use cleaning products with extreme caution on heirlooms such as this quilt. In most cases, seek professional help for both routine care and special problems.

riatic acid and oxalic acid) have a caustic or corrosive effect on tissue.

Combustible, flammable, and extremely flammable. These terms are used in precautionary labeling to designate the likelihood that a material will catch fire. The definition of each term is based on the material's flash point—the temperature reached by the material before a spark will cause the vapor to ignite. Gasoline and acetone are extremely flammable. Many alcohols are flammable. Kerosene is combustible. It is not safe to store extremely flammable materials for any length of time; when storing them, be sure to keep them well away from heat sources, and in tightly covered metal containers.

Lubricants. Lubricating substances, as defined here, are those substances that reduce friction between two surfaces or that soften a stain so that it is easier to remove. Lubricants include oils, powdered graphite, petroleum jelly, silicone spray, lanolin, and glycerine.

Solvents. Solvents are liquids that dissolve other substances, forming a solution that can be washed off. Acetone, alcohol, dry-cleaning fluids, paint thinners, and water are all solvents.

Toxic and poisonous. Chemicals that can make you ill if ingested, inhaled, or absorbed through the skin are called *toxic.* Toxic chemicals that can cause death when small doses are ingested are called *poisonous.* Highly toxic chemicals require that a skull and crossbones and the word "Poison" be marked on the label. *Always* read the label for cautions before using any household product.

HOME SAFETY

Conduct a quick check around your house for dangerous chemicals (see Household Products, pages 10–15) and other items. The most common causes of home accidents, statistically speaking, are stairs, nails, tacks and screws, furniture, glass doors and windows, tools, playground equipment, cutlery, swimming pools, ladders, and fences.

Check for fire dangers as well. Make certain that everyone in the house knows the quickest ways to exit, that your smoke detectors and fire extinguishers are in good working order, and that combustible materials are stored safely. Keep your electrical and heating systems in top condition (see pages 82–83 and 86–88). Use the list below as a guide for your room-to-room safety check.

Living areas
1. Stairways should be lighted, wall switches at both ends.
2. Carpeting should be tacked down.
3. Handrails on stairs should be secure.
4. Hard floors should have no-skid waxes and rugs.
5. Sliding glass doors should be marked with decals.
6. Second-floor windows should have secure screens.
7. Fireplace should be screened.
8. Observe safety precautions included with portable heaters.

Basic First-Aid Kit

Absorbent-cotton roll	Large gauze pads
Adhesive pads	Motion-sickness tablets
Adhesive tape	Oval eye-pads
Antiseptic wipes	Petroleum jelly
Aspirin	(for chapped skin)
A variety of bandages:	Rubbing alcohol
□ 1-in.-wide sheer strip	(for sore muscles
bandages	and as a disinfectant)
□ Triangular bandage (for	Safety pins
broken arm or shoulder)	Scissors
□ 3-in.-wide elastic bandage	Spirits of ammonia
□ Variety of gauze bandages	capsules (for fainting)
(1 in. to 2 in.)	Sunburn lotion
Calamine lotion	Syrup of ipecac
Cotton balls	(to induce vomiting)
Cotton swabs (Q-tips)	Thermometers
First-aid cream	Tourniquet
	Tweezers

Bathrooms
1. Door should have outside-lock release.
2. Floors should be kept dry and covered.
3. Outlets should be grounded (see Electrical Systems, pages 82–83).
4. Medicines should be kept in locked cabinets and out of reach of children.
5. Tubs, showers should have grab bars and rubber mats.
6. First-aid kit should be kept handy and up to date.

Kitchen
1. Appliances should be grounded (see Electrical Systems, pages 82–83).
2. Fire extinguishers should be kept handy for electrical, trash, and grease fires. Consult your local fire department business office for guidelines.
3. Cleaners and chemicals should be kept in locked cabinets and out of reach of children.

Workshop, garage, and basement
1. Outlets should be grounded (see Electrical Systems, pages 82–83).
2. Tools should be kept in locked cabinets and out of reach of children.
3. Combustibles should be stored away from heat sources and in metal containers.
4. Heating and cooling systems should be kept in good repair (see Heating and Cooling Systems, pages 86–88).
5. Storage should be kept to a minimum.
6. Garage door should be opened before you warm up the car.
7. Guns, ammunition, and fireworks should be kept in locked cabinets and out of reach of children.

Outside
1. Porches, paths, and steps should be lighted.
2. Pool should be fenced.
3. Ladders should be used safely (never use aluminum ladders around electrical sources).
4. Walks and steps should be kept clear of ice and snow.

Emergencies
In an emergency, preparation and awareness save lives. It is better to do nothing than the wrong thing. Below are some ways to prepare for emergencies.
1. Take a first-aid course if possible, or keep a basic first-aid book handy.
2. Keep emergency procedures for fires and weather emergencies handy. Your local fire and safety agencies will provide this information free of charge.
3. Keep fire, police, doctor, and ambulance telephone numbers posted near the phone. Include your own address and phone number in case a visitor or babysitter needs to let emergency services know where your house is.
4. Do not move or treat an injured person unless you are certain you know what you are doing, or are following a doctor's instructions.
5. When you move to a new area, find and be familiar with the quickest route to a hospital emergency ward.

HOME SECURITY

To make your home an undesirable target for burglars, follow the guidelines below.

1. Install adequate outdoor lighting, especially above doorways and around secluded windows.

2. When possible, trim shrubs and avoid fences to keep windows and doors in view of the street and neighbors.

3. Keep sliding-glass-door locks and window locks in good condition (see Doors, Woodwork, and Windows, pages 32–33). Security devices should not keep you from exiting quickly in case of fire.

4. Install deadbolt locks on all exterior doors. The newest deadbolt locks have important new safety features.

5. Keep your house keys with you—burglars know most of the possible hiding places.

6. Install a wide-angle peephole in your front door.

Before you go on vacation or leave a vacation home, check the list below for ways to make the house look occupied.

1. Cancel newspaper and mail deliveries.

2. Install automatic timers to turn lights on and off at normal hours, and to turn on a radio periodically during the day and evening.

3. Do not announce your vacation plans to the press—burglars check the papers for just such information.

4. Turn your telephone down so the ring cannot be heard.

5. Ask a neighbor to park a car in your driveway occasionally, to open and close drapes as you would do, and to check your home as often as possible.

6. Leave your itinerary and telephone numbers with the local police department and with a neighbor.

Security Devices

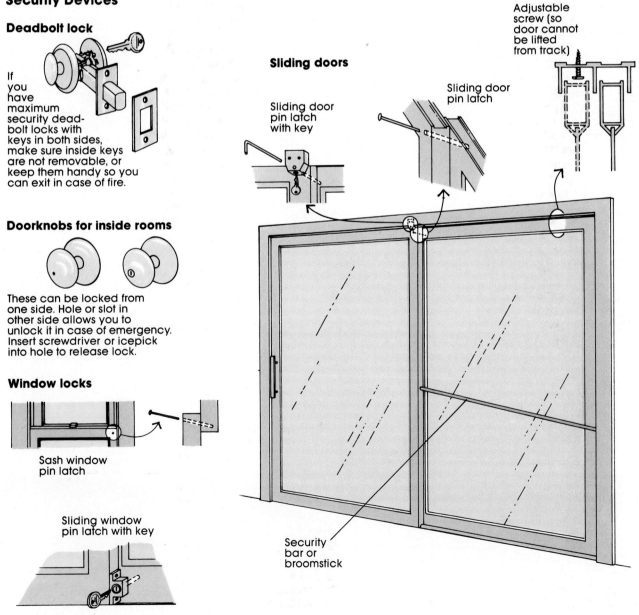

Deadbolt lock

If you have maximum security deadbolt locks with keys in both sides, make sure inside keys are not removable, or keep them handy so you can exit in case of fire.

Doorknobs for inside rooms

These can be locked from one side. Hole or slot in other side allows you to unlock it in case of emergency. Insert screwdriver or icepick into hole to release lock.

Window locks

Sash window pin latch

Sliding window pin latch with key

Sliding doors

Sliding door pin latch with key

Sliding door pin latch

Adjustable screw (so door cannot be lifted from track)

Security bar or broomstick

YOUR HOME'S INTERIOR

Knowing how to care for
all the surfaces, materials,
and items inside your home is
one of the keys to a beautiful
environment. This chapter
provides the information you
need to care for your home
with confidence.

Home care and upkeep isn't a single event—it's the ongoing process of refining and caring for your environment so you can enjoy it more. From washing the dishes to adding on a room, the care you put into your home and its contents can greatly enhance your life. In addition, most rooms make an immediate impression on people, consciously or unconsciously. Whether the room has off-white walls, pale green carpet and lucite furniture, or wood-paneled walls, oriental carpets, and antique furniture, its general state of order, cleanliness, and beauty are apparent.

Part of this impression has to do with design. A room looks and feels better when it serves its function. Furniture arrangement, storage facilities, and lighting all create an effect. If you want your living room to be a place in which to relax, you can arrange the furniture so that it's clearly not a major traffic way, create intimate and subdued lighting, and place in it only those items suited to quiet activities or social occasions. (For more information, see Ortho's *How to Design & Build Storage Projects*.)

Color and style are a matter of choice, but these choices are often influenced by care and maintenance issues. People often limit themselves to dark, dirt-hiding colors and tough, durable fabrics because they aren't sure how to keep lighter colors and flimsier fabrics clean. But when you know how to take care of a wide variety of materials, fabrics, and surfaces, you can choose exactly those colors and fabrics you like best, even if that means pale-colored carpets and silk wallcoverings. It's easy to take care of the most elegant interior when you know how. This chapter shows you how to clean and protect the surfaces and possessions inside your house. Each section is organized into three parts: *routine care*—jobs done weekly, such as vacuuming and dusting; *periodic care*—jobs done once a month or once a year, such as waxing floors or cleaning walls; and *special problems*—occasional jobs, such as repairing a scratch in wood floors

or furniture, oiling a sticking door-lock, or removing stains from wallpaper.

The tools, equipment, and household products mentioned in this chapter are discussed fully in the first chapter. If you have a question about a product (especially when cautions are involved), refer to "Household Products," pages 10–15. When you are buying a new tool or piece of equipment, or looking for a particular household product, read the accompanying literature or labels very carefully. Manufacturers give as many practical guidelines as possible for the use of their products, and are required by law to inform you of the precautions to follow when using those products.

A series of resource charts appears in mid-chapter. The Fabric Care chart (pages 38–41) tells whether a fabric should be dry cleaned or washed, how to dry and iron it, and which laundry and stain-removing products to use. The 10-page Stain chart (pages 42–51) lists specific stains you may find on washable and non-washable fabrics, carpets, and upholstery, and tells you how to remove them. If you get a coffee stain on your clothing and your upholstered chair at the same time, use the Fabric Care chart and the Stain chart to take care of both problems. The Household Items and Surfaces section on pages 52–61 covers the care of hundreds of different materials around your house, from alabaster to zinc, and from bathtubs to venetian blinds. Special problems appear in italics so you can find them easily. The Appliances section (pages 62–65) discusses some of the common repairs to large and small appliances you can do yourself. It contains simple illustrations of blenders, mixers, and vacuum cleaners to help you identify the interior parts mentioned in the text. The Pests section on pages 66–69 helps you identify various household pests and tells you how to eliminate them. The Odors section on pages 70–71 tells you what you can use to create refreshing scents or to eliminate annoying household odors. Finally, page 71 offers guidelines for coping with household problems related to pets—fleas, scratched furniture, and so on. Whatever your needs may be, you'll find guidelines for common and not-so-common home-care issues on these next 52 pages.

The feeling of warmth and comfort in a room is achieved not only through its basic design, but through the daily care and attention that is given to it.

CARPETS & RUGS

Mats

Of all the areas in your house, floors take the biggest beating. Much of the outside dirt gets tracked in and transferred to other parts of your house. To prevent the influx of dirt into your house, place mats both inside and outside all exterior doors. Inside, use a transparent commercial carpet mat that is almost as wide as the doorway; or use an extra piece of carpeting, backed with rubber or vinyl to keep it from sliding around. Outside, there are many kinds of matting to choose from—coconut, rush, or synthetic. Here too, make certain that the matting is as wide as or wider than the doorway, and that it can't slide around. It is much easier to clean these mats than to constantly deal with accumulated dust and dirt. Sweep or vacuum them often. Occasionally take them up and sweep or vacuum the floor or doorway underneath. Place strips of matting or rubber-backed carpet in hallways and heavy traffic areas—they will make your floor cleaning easier, and protect your floors from damage as well.

Routine care

All carpets require the same kind of routine care: regular vacuuming. Vacuum heavy traffic areas daily, if possible. Vacuum all areas thoroughly at least once a week, going over each five or six times. Be sure to pick up pins, clips, and other hard or large objects before vacuuming to protect your vacuum from unnecessary damage. Remove spots and stains as soon as they happen. Vacuum the backing and padding occasionally to prevent dirt

Fibers

As a general rule, the denser the pile, the better carpets will wear. Deep pile gives better wear than short, with the exception of shag. Because shag carpets have widely spaced tufts, they tend to wear unevenly. It is especially important not to overwet deep pile and shag carpets during deep cleaning—when wet, exposed backing materials can cause stains on the fibers, and damage the floor. If you don't know what fiber your carpet is made of, try this quick test. Cut off a small piece of fiber and set a match to it. If it beads up, it is a synthetic, if it burns to an ash, it is wool or cotton (wool will have a stronger odor than cotton).

Type of fiber	Comments
Wool	Wears well, but can be difficult to clean because detergent alkalis can harm animal fibers; therefore, only mild detergents can be used on wool. Wool also tends to hold moisture and can mildew, so do not overwet during cleaning. To avoid shrinkage, make sure the temperature of the water during steam cleaning does not exceed 150°F. Wool carpets should be mothproofed by the manufacturer.
Nylon	Noted for its durability, nylon is relatively easy to clean and rates high on colorfastness. It tends to attract static, but may be treated with an antistatic agent or may contain fibers that will neutralize these charges. Nylon can also pill (the fibers can form fuzz).
Acrylics	Generally regarded as having good wearability and excellent resistance to soiling. May tend to retain oily soils. Generally easy to clean.
Polyester	Resists abrasion very well. May not clean as easily as other synthetics and can retain oily soils. Some may be static-prone.
Polypropylene olefins	Found in indoor-outdoor carpets, this fiber wears well and resists soiling.

Padding

Padding—also called cushion, underlay, or lining—helps absorb some of the wear your carpet receives. Thicker padding is appropriate for heavy traffic areas, over concrete floors, or in creating a sense of luxury. Padding is commonly made of hair, jute, soft rubber, or various types of plastics. Hair padding generally does the best job of protecting your carpeting but, like jute and soft rubber, it can be easily damaged or mildewed. Solvent cleaners can harm rubber, and some plastics give off thick smoke and toxic gas when ignited.

Backing

Carpet backing can be made of jute, latex, thermoplastics, foam or sponge rubber, cotton, rayon, or synthetics. Latex and rubber can be harmed by solvent-type cleaners, and jute tends to mildew if left wet for too long. Whenever you are deep cleaning carpets, remember that the cleaning method and agent affect the backing as well as the carpet fibers.

from becoming embedded in the fibers and filtering through to the floor.

The more you can keep carpets and rugs free of surface dirt and atmospheric oils, the longer they will last and the better they will look. The newest carpet fibers are designed to hide dirt and resist liquids, but embedded oils and grit can quickly dull the colors and may eventually cut through rug fibers. Remember that the same dust and dirt you can see on hard floors is also settling into your carpet. Remove it with the same regularity as for other types of floors.

Vacuum cleaners

To ensure a long life for your carpets, invest in a good-quality vacuum cleaner—one with a beater brush as well as good suction. Many professionals recommend a wet-dry vacuum, which you can use on *all* your floors (wet or dry), and for vacuuming drapes, furniture, and so on. Although they are priced in the same range as any good vacuum, they are more versatile—consider buying one if you're in the market for a new vacuum cleaner. There are also two vacuums you might consider: a strong upright for central areas, and a cannister with attachments for corners, crevices, furniture, stairways, and so on.

Periodic care

Deep clean all your carpets and rugs once a year. You may choose from several methods, described on the right. You can do the cleaning yourself or hire a professional. Because your carpets represent a considerable investment, you may prefer to have them cleaned professionally.

Professional cleaning: Be sure to find a reputable, bonded, and insured company that is willing to guarantee its work. Ask your friends for referrals first, then check the Yellow Pages.

1. Ask what methods and chemicals they use. Ask how toxic the chemical is, especially if you have crawling babies or family members who are sensitive to chemicals.

2. If they use a dry compound or a solution that dries to a powder, ask them if they remove all of it. Any residue will quickly attract dirt.

3. If they use water in their cleaning method, ask how long it will take for the carpet to dry. It may be longer than you want to wait.

4. If they use a water/extraction method, ask what percentage of the water and chemical will be removed. It should be at least 85 to 95 percent.

5. When you are satisfied with the method, describe the type and size of your carpet, and any special stains or problems, such as odors. With this information they should be able to give you a reasonably close cost estimate.

Do-it-yourself: You can rent equipment from many supermarkets and rental agencies. Carefully read both the literature accompanying the machine and the labels on the cleaning solutions. Make sure the method is compatible with your carpet fibers (see chart on page 20). As you clean, try not to get the carpet too wet.

Deep-cleaning methods

There are advantages and disadvantages to all deep-cleaning methods. Read through the descriptions of each of the four primary methods and choose the one that seems best suited to your carpet.

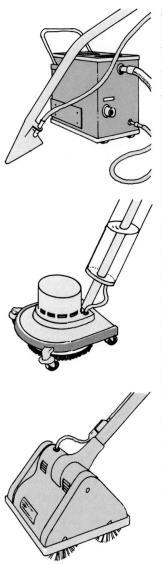

Steam/extraction
Machines inject water and a chemical cleaner into the carpet and remove it almost simultaneously through an opening in the same nozzle. Water over 150°F can damage wool carpets and may take the twist out of fibers. Make sure at least 85 to 95 percent of the moisture is removed. If the carpet is left too wet, it may mildew or quickly resoil, and the floor could be damaged.

Shampooing
Water- or solvent-based chemical foam is applied to the carpet, agitated, allowed to dry, and vacuumed up. The rotary floor machines generally used with this method may damage plush, shag, cut-and-loop, or frieze (twist) carpets. Unless almost all of the foam and dirt are removed, they will remain in the carpet and attract more dirt.

Dry cleaning
The carpet is misted with solvent and sprinkled with an absorbent cleaning material, then brushed and vacuumed. Large amounts of the absorbent can remain in the carpet and attract dirt unless a very strong vacuum is used.

Yarn bonnet
This method is designed to remove surface soil frequently to *avoid* deep cleaning. It employs a rotating disc using cotton pads moistened with a carpet-cleaning solution. *Or* the carpet may be sprayed with a carbonated water solution before scrubbing with the machine. The pads absorb the cleaner and the surface dirt.

Vacuum oriental carpets and other delicate rugs on both sides to prevent sand and grit from cutting the fibers.

Delicate rugs

Some area rugs require special care and should not be cleaned along with your carpets. For precautions, see the comments below.

Oriental and silk

In general, do not risk cleaning these rugs yourself—they are delicate. If yours are valuable, always have them cleaned and repaired professionally by a rug-cleaning specialist. Vacuum or shake them often to keep dirt from damaging rug fibers. If the fringe becomes heavily soiled, scrub it with a soft brush, using lukewarm, soapy water; then rinse it with clear water. Squeeze out the excess moisture with a towel, and comb the fringe out gently with your fingers. If you want to clean the rug yourself, one way is to lay it face-down for a few hours on fresh snow—the snow will absorb the dirt. Then dry it face-up on top of towels in a warm room. Do not steam-clean wool oriental rugs—the heat used can cause them to shrink. To protect them from carpet beetles and moths, place small cloth bags of moth crystals underneath (but not if you have small children in the house—moth crystals are poisonous).

Fur

Fur must be protected from insects. Shake or sweep fur rugs daily to discourage infestation. To eliminate pests, see Pest section, pages 66 to 69. Clean by sprinkling with coarse cornmeal, then brush and shake well. If rugs are very soiled or odorous, take them to a professional rug cleaner.

Braided and hooked

Most of these rugs have fabric backings. Never shake or beat them, or they may separate from the base. Sweep or vacuum them often, on both sides. When they get faded or are badly soiled, take them to a professional rug cleaner.

Numdah rugs

These delicate rugs from India, made of matted goat's hair, must never be shaken, beaten, or brushed. Vacuum both sides at least once a week. When they get soiled, take them to a professional rug cleaner.

Special problems

In addition to routine and periodic cleaning, you may sometimes run into special problems, such as spots and stains, burns, carpet moths, odors, pilling, and so on. The information below will help you cope with these occasional problems.

Buckles: Wrinkles in carpeting can be caused by faulty installation, overwetting, or stretching (due to heavy objects being dragged across it). Since the carpeting may have to be restretched to correct the problem, it is a good idea to ask your dealer to take a look at it.

Burns: For surface burns, snip off damaged fiber ends, use a sponge to clean the area with a detergent solution, then rinse off and blot dry. Deeper burns need to be cut out and replaced. See Ortho's book, *Basic Home Repairs*, for instructions on cutting in a carpet patch.

Crushing or matting: To restore an area crushed by furniture legs, apply a clean, damp cloth to the area, steam lightly with a warm iron, and then brush up the nap.

Curling: Roll the curled edge of a rug in the opposite direction, hold it, place a cloth over it, steam with an iron, and then flatten out the curl with your hand.

Fuzzing or shedding: This is a common problem with new wools and some synthetic carpets. The best way to deal with it is just to vacuum.

Loose ends of fibers: This problem may be caused by sharp edges on the vacuum, or by sharp high heels. Never pull on a loose end—just cut it off.

Moths: If your wool carpeting did not receive a moth-resistant treatment during its manufacture, check it occasionally for this pest. You can try dealing with the problem yourself (see the Pests section, pages 66 to 69), or call a professional.

Odors: To remove chemicals and synthetic odors, mustiness, and pet odors, sprinkle the area with an absorbent such as baking soda or cornstarch. Let the powder stand, then vacuum it up. Commercial carpet-deodorizers are available from grocery stores and pet shops.

Pilling: This may be caused by a vacuum that is set too low to the floor, or by a damaged vacuum nozzle. Carefully snip off pills or tiny balls and, when possible, use an upright cleaner with beater brushes.

Spots and stains: Act as quickly as possible. Vacuum or blot up as much of the material as possible. Sponge with cold water. If, however, the spill is a greasy or oily one, soak it up with an absorbent such as baking soda or cornstarch. Test stain-removing agents on an inconspicuous area of the carpet before using to make certain they don't harm the dyes or fibers. See pages 42 to 51 for treating common spots and stains.

WOOD FLOORS

Most wood floors actually have several layers: the bare wood; a sealer that penetrates the wood and seals its "pores"; a surface finish such as varnish, shellac, lacquer, or polyurethane; and a coat of wax or oil, which protects these other layers. Routine care of wood floors consists of keeping this wax or oil coating in good condition; periodic care consists of renewing it. Given a regular program of such care, your wood floors should remain in beautiful condition for years.

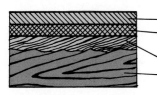

- Wax, polish, or oil
- Finish (varnish, lacquer, shellac, polyurethane)
- Penetrating sealer
- Bare wood

Painted wood floors generally should be waxed and treated just like regular wood finishes. However, avoid any kind of abrasive cleansers, and do not use scrubbing or buffing machines. If you need to touch up or repaint, remove all the wax first with a commercial wax stripper. Oiled wood floors require a slightly different maintenance approach—see the box on this page.

If your wood floor is currently in good shape, you can simply continue whatever routine was used in the past. If you don't know what that routine was, select a cleaning agent and wax you like and follow the procedures outlined below. If your floor is currently in bad shape, see the section on Special Problems on the next page.

Routine care

1. Dust mop as frequently as necessary and practical with an *unoiled* mop—oil ruins wax. Dust mops pick up more than brooms, so they provide better protection from the grit that dulls wax and ruins finishes. Shake the mop outside, or into a paper bag.

2. Remove spots, marks, or stains as soon as they happen. See the Special Problems section on the next page.

3. If the floor needs more than dust mopping but you don't want to wax it, mop with a sponge mop squeezed almost dry with clear, lukewarm water. (The taboo against using water on wood is to protect the wood itself, not the wax. But be sure to use warm, not hot, water—hot water dissolves wax.) If you generally use a water-based liquid polish, add a little to the water.

Oiled wood

Your floor may be oiled instead of waxed. Some people prefer this softer look. If possible, clean daily with an oiled dust mop. Mop when necessary with a solution of very mild detergent and lukewarm water, then dry thoroughly. Apply a new coat of oil by warming a can or jar of paraffin oil *or* boiled linseed oil, wipe up any excess, and apply further coats as desired. If you prefer a wax finish, simply clean the floor and apply the wax.

It's important to keep a protective coat of wax, polish, or oil on wood floors; otherwise, dirt and grit will eventually abrade the finish. (**Top,** hardwood floor; **left,** stenciled wood; **right,** parquet wood.)

Periodic care

When the present coat of wax gets dull, rewax the floor. Depending on how heavily trafficked the floor is, and what type of wax you use, you may need to wax as often as once a month, or as seldom as two times a year. If you keep your floor clean and wax only in heavily trafficked areas where wax is really necessary, your floor won't suffer from too much "waxy build-up," and you won't have to remove wax very often. But if a new coat of wax doesn't give your floor the shine you want, or if the floor just doesn't look as clean as you'd like, remove the old wax before you apply a new coat. To remove wax, follow the steps described on page 25.

WOOD FLOORS

Choosing waxes and polishes

Because of the difference in hardness, porosity, and types of floor materials, there is a variety of protective products. Always check the label to determine which waxes or polishes are best to use on your floors.

Paste wax

Paste waxes are generally thought to be the best waxes for wood because they are more durable than most liquid products. Their ability to seal small cracks makes them especially good on older wood floors. Remove pastes with a solvent once a year to avoid waxy build-up and yellowing (see photographs on page 25). All paste waxes must be buffed to remove excess wax and to bring up the shine. You can buff by hand, but it is easier to rent a floor machine. Purchase an extra set of felt pads for the final buffing—the better the buffing job, the harder the wax. If you have very large areas to wax, consider purchasing a buffing machine, which you can also use to renew the shine between waxings. Paste waxes work on vinyl floors, but are not recommended and should not be used on linoleum, rubber, cork, or asphalt. They generally are too slippery for use on masonry floors.

Liquid wax and polish

A wide range of liquid products is available for use on all types of floors. Water-based liquids are not recommended for wood or cork floors—use solvent-based waxes instead. Remove the wax or polish every six to eight months, or whenever the floor begins to look dull. You don't need to buff self-polishing liquids, although you can buff them lightly to bring up a higher shine.

Self-cleaning liquid polish

Products in this category contain a cleaning agent that removes the previous layer of wax with each application. They usually are self-polishing as well, so you don't have to buff. Layers will still build up. Remove after six to eight applications, and reapply. Do not use for wood or cork floors unless the label specifically indicates such use—the cleaning agents may damage the finish.

Special problems

If your wood floor is in bad shape, you must diagnose the problem. If the problem is structural—sloping floors, warped or squeaking boards, and so on—refer to Ortho's book, *Basic Home Repairs,* to correct the problem. If the floor's appearance is what's wrong, work down through the layers to find the source of the problem—the wax, the finish, or the wood itself. Once you have found the problem, remove all the old wax. Then, if problem spots remain, try removing them as instructed in the following copy. If they still remain, you may have to remove the old floor finish and apply a new one. Seek professional advice for this. If your floor still looks bad—which usually occurs only in cases of severe neglect or damage—you may need to resand the entire floor. Seek professional advice for this job.

Alcohol or water marks: Rub with fine steel wool and floor polish *or* wax. If the mark persists, rub with steel wool and odorless mineral spirits. Wash and rewax.

Black heel marks: Rub with fine steel wool and floor polish or wax.

Burn marks: For minor burns, sand lightly, wash, dry, and rewax. For deeper burns, clean the area and carefully scrape out all the blackened wood with a sharp knife. If very little wood was lost, retouch the spot with commercial scratch hider or crayon (available at hardware stores). You may need two coats. Rewax and buff. Treat a deep burn hole as you would a gouge.

How to wax

1. If you can, move the furniture out of the room. Otherwise, move it to the middle and wax the edges; then move it to the edges and wax the middle.
2. Using a large cloth, rag mop, or wax applicator, spread the wax on 3-foot areas at a time. If using paste wax, apply a second coat to heavy traffic areas. Apply only one coat under large area rugs (to reduce danger of slipping).
3. Buff by hand *or* with a buffing machine (available from most rental agencies). Follow the grain of the wood. Labels generally advise that you allow paste wax to dry completely before buffing, and buff liquid waxes while they are still damp.

Chewing gum, wax, crayon, or tar: Harden material with ice. Scrape up with a spatula. Rub remaining material with fine steel wool and odorless mineral spirits. Rewax.

Dark spots (caused by standing water, cleaners, or urine): Remove wax or polish with TSP *or* a commercial wax stripper. Wash with vinegar, and allow to soak in; then wipe dry. Repeat, if necessary. If spot still remains, apply 1 tbsp oxalic acid crystals dissolved in 1 c water. Allow to soak until spot disappears; then wipe up with a damp cloth and rinse well. (Oxalic acid is a corrosive, poisonous bleach that will remove the finish and possibly the sealer. See page 14 for precautions needed when using this chemical.) To ensure that the sealer is still in the wood, sprinkle with a few drops of water. If it beads up, the sealer is undamaged. If the drops soak into the wood, reseal with a wood sealer, then refinish with the appropriate wood stain. Rewax.

Grease or oil spills: Wipe up immediately. Sponge with liquid detergent straight from the bottle. Sprinkle with baking soda and leave on overnight. Wash with a general household cleaner containing ammonia. Rewax.

How to remove wax

1. Use a commercial wax stripper made for wood floors. For other types of floors, use a solution of 1 gal warm water, 1 c ammonia, and ½ c TSP (for marble floors, see box on page 27). Apply solution to the floor, and let it soak in for a few minutes. Then scrub with a brush or floor polisher.
2. Wipe up solution with a sponge or sponge mop, *or* scrape into a dustpan with a floor squeegee (available at janitorial-supply houses) or an old window squeegee.
3. Rinse with clean water, *or* vacuum with a wet-dry cleaner, and allow to dry thoroughly before rewaxing.

Scratches and gouges

1. Small scratches do not usually show up under a good layer of wax. If the scratch is fairly deep, try a commercial scratch hider or crayon (available at hardware stores) that matches the color of your floor.
2. Deep scratches and gouges can be filled with wood filler matched to the color of your floor. Clean the area to remove all the wax or oil. Then fill the gouge.
3. When filler is set, sand smooth, and wax *or* oil. You can create a perfectly matched wood filler by making a paste of sawdust from a spare floorboard and wood glue.

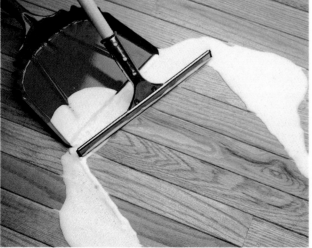

RESILIENT FLOORS

Resilient, or pliable, flooring includes all types of vinyl floorings as well as linoleum, rubber, cork, and asphalt. The last four types generally are found only in older homes. Most of the resilient flooring in modern homes is made of vinyl. Caring for your floor is quite simple: Routine care generally consists of dust-mopping or sweeping, and occasional damp-mopping with clear water. Periodically apply a protective finish, such as vinyl floor polish or wax, to protect the floor and keep up the shine. When the floor begins to look dull in spite of waxing or polishing, it's time to strip off all the layers of wax or polish and start over. (See page 25 for how to remove wax.) Instead of washing and waxing separately, you can try a liquid self-cleaning polish; it is easy to use, but the finish is less durable than some of the other waxes and polishes. Always wipe up spills as quickly as possible to avoid stains. Periodic care and protective finishes for specific types of resilient floors are listed below.

To damp mop, prepare two buckets, one with your cleaning solution, one with fresh rinsing water. Using a sponge or rag mop, wipe 3-foot sections. Then rinse with the clean water, wiping up the solution and dirt as you go.

Type of Floor	Routine Care	Periodic Care	Comments
No-wax vinyl	Mop with warm water only; water and a mild detergent; *or* water mixed with a no-wax floor finish.	No wax necessary. May be polished with commercial no-wax finish.	Heat sensitive.
Vinyl and vinyl asbestos	Mop with water-based polish *or* mild detergent and water. Strip and re-polish every 6 to 8 washings.	Wax with water-based floor polish.	Heat sensitive. Avoid abrasive scouring pads and powder, acetone (nail polish remover).
Linoleum	Mop with water and a mild detergent. Wash no more often than necessary—water eventually hardens linoleum.	Wax frequently with a water-based polish.	Avoid strong alkalis such as washing soda, and abrasive scouring pads and powders. May be painted.
Asphalt tile	Mop with water and mild detergent.	Wax with a water-based wax or polish.	Avoid solvents, grease, and abrasive scouring pads and powder.
Rubber tile	Mop with water and mild detergent, *or* water mixed with water-based floor polish.	Wax frequently with a water-based polish.	Heat sensitive. Avoid oil, grease, and solvents such as turpentine or alcohol. Do not use paste wax.
Natural cork	Sweep or vacuum frequently.	Wax with a solvent-based polish.	Avoid caustic (lye, chlorine) and alkali (washing soda) cleaners.

Special problems
Just as with wood floors, resilient floors also benefit from mats that are placed on both sides of your exterior doors. These mats keep sand and grit from dulling resilient floor coverings.

To remove stubborn stains: Stubborn stains can often be removed with a detergent paste, your usual floor polish, *or* with ammonia *or* vinegar. Wipe up these cleaners quickly to avoid damaging the floor's finish. Before using chemicals, test them in an inconspicuous place, such as inside a closet. Remove black heel marks with an ink-pen eraser.

To remove chewing gum and paint: Scrape up as much as possible with a spatula or dull knife. Remove what remains with a small amount of dry-cleaning fluid or paint thinner. (Don't use solvents on rubber tile.)

To remove scratches and gouges: For deep scratches and gouges on unpatterned floors, use a sharp knife to scrape off flakes from an extra tile or from an inconspicuous place. Chop or grind the scrapings into a fine powder and mix with white glue, clear nail polish, *or* shellac until the mix is thick and pasty. Surround the damaged area with strips of masking tape, and smooth the paste into the spot with a putty knife. When dry, sand smooth with fine steel wool. Restore the shine with clear nail polish, if necessary. If the damage is too large, or the pattern difficult to match, you may have to replace the section. Consult Ortho's book, *Basic Home Repairs* for techniques for replacing tile.

To remove bubbles: These generally are caused by poor installation, or by damp subflooring. Soften the area by covering it with a piece of aluminum foil, and ironing with a warm iron. Slit the bubble with a sharp knife or razor blade, following the pattern. (Check underneath for the cause of the problem. If the underflooring is damp, leave the slit open long enough for it to dry.) Force some mastic or white glue under the slit, and press flat. Remove the excess glue with hot water, or remove the mastic with paint thinner. Then weight the flooring down overnight with books or furniture.

MASONRY FLOORS

Masonry floors are easy to maintain, although some are prone to staining because of their porosity. Most are sealed with masonry sealer (except for unglazed tile.) If your floor is not sealed, consider having it done professionally. *Or* do it yourself with a sealer (available at hardware stores). Waxing is generally not recommended: A matte-finish floor will be covered by the wax, whereas terrazzo and ceramic tile cannot hold the wax but transfers it onto shoes, which in turn transfer it onto the surrounding carpet or wood floors. If you do wax, do not overbuff the floor or it will become dangerously slippery. However, waxing a cement floor in the garage or basement is beneficial—the wax helps keep down cement dust, which would otherwise be brought into the house on people's shoes. Never use wax around fireplaces, wood stoves, or anywhere else it will be affected by heat. When scrubbing a masonry floor, follow the grain to avoid scratches.

To remove stains from marble, make a paste of marble cleaning flakes and hydrogen peroxide. Rub gently with the grain, rinse with a mild vinegar solution, then immediately rinse off the vinegar with water and dry thoroughly.

Type of Floor	Routine Care	Periodic Care	Comments
Quarry tile, slate, and flagstone	Clean with water and washing soda, *or* a mild detergent solution.	Wax with a water-based wax or polish.	Vacuum thoroughly before cleaning to avoid soil from building up in the cracks. Avoid acids such as vinegar and fruit juices, and abrasive pads and powders.
Glazed ceramic tile	Mop with water and washing soda, *or* a mild detergent solution.	May be too slippery if waxed. Restore shine by polishing with a buffing machine, *or* by hand.	Avoid acids such as vinegar and fruit juices.
Terrazzo	Mop with water only, *or* with a solution of water and mild detergent.	Wax with a water- or solvent-based wax or polish.	Avoid acids such as vinegar and fruit juices, abrasive pads, and powders.
Brick and cement	Clean with water and washing soda, *or* TSP, *or* a detergent solution. Use a rag mop—sponge mops will break apart on rough floors.	Wax with a water-based wax if the floor is sealed.	If the floor is not sealed, consider having it done professionally. *Or* do it yourself with a masonry sealer (available at hardware stores).

Marble

Mop polished marble with a mild solution of soap flakes (preferably made especially for cleaning marble) and water. Because it is a luxury floor finish, take some special care to maintain its beauty. Unless it is well sealed—a job for professionals—it tends to be too porous to withstand stains well. It is especially vulnerable to acids such as vinegar and fruit juices, and alcohol. These can etch its surface, making it look whitish and dull. To remove stains, make a thick paste of your cleaning flakes and hydrogen peroxide. Rub the paste on the stain with the grain, then rinse off. For rust stains, use a commercial rust remover. Stain removing may etch the surface; if so, polish with whiting (available at home improvement centers). The floor can be waxed with a paste wax and buffed with a floor polisher. But for best results, have a professional do the waxing and buffing. Do not use alkaline cleaning solutions, such as washing soda or ammonia, on marble—they will break up and dull the surface. These instructions for marble floors apply to marble furniture as well, although you will be buffing by hand, of course.

Special problems

The following are directions for handling problems on brick, cement, ceramic tile, flagstone, slate, and terrazzo.

To remove stains: Make a thick paste of washing soda *or* TSP and water, and apply to the spot. Leave until paste is dry, then rinse off. Repeat until the stain is gone. If stain remains, rub with fine steel wool and a water-based, self-cleaning wax. For stains that have penetrated deeply into the stone itself, use oxalic acid, a strong chemical bleach available at hardware stores. Follow label directions carefully—it is a corrosive poison. After removing a stain, a white film may remain from the chemicals or cleaning solution used; if so, rinse with equal parts vinegar and water, then rinse quickly with plain water to avoid etching the surface. If the stain remover has etched the surface, rub with fine steel wool or a paste of whiting (available at home improvement centers) and water. Rub with the grain, not in circles. To remove stains and mildew on grout, scrub with scouring powder containing chlorine bleach, using a grout brush.

You may think of cleaning your walls only when they become visibly soiled. However, routine care will lengthen the life of all types of walls and wall coverings, and allow you more time between overall cleanings. Whenever possible, ask your home-improvement-center dealer for guidelines on the techniques and products suitable for your particular paint and wall coverings. When you buy new wall coverings, purchase extra to test cleaning products, make minor repairs, and help you coordinate colors and textures when you decorate.

Routine care
Dust and vacuum the cobwebs and dust from your walls regularly. If you don't, the dirt will mix with moisture and smoke in the air, and create a grime that may be impossible to remove. Use a lamb's-wool duster, cloth-wrapped broom, or the brush attachment of your vacuum cleaner. (Extension handles for dusters are available from hardware stores.) At the same time use a damp sponge to spot clean around light fixtures, doorknobs, window sills, heating vents, and woodwork.

Periodic care
Ideally, wall surfaces should be cleaned overall once every couple of years. Move all the furniture to the center of the room, and cover it and the floors with drop cloths. Take down pictures, removable shelves, and curtains or drapes. If it is too difficult to remove and replace the drapes, pull them out from the windows, drape them over chairs, and cover them with drop cloths. Clean the ceiling first—see Ceilings on page 31. Dust or vacuum the walls thoroughly, and treat any special problems (such as stains) before cleaning. An effective and safe cleaner for all types of walls and ceilings is a chemically treated sponge called a "dry sponge" (available at some janitorial-supply houses and home-improvement centers). The sponge is meant to be used as is, without water. Buy the largest one available, and fold it so that it has several surfaces. Once it is saturated with grime, it can be washed and used as a wet sponge. Follow the guidelines below for specific cleaning solutions and for special problems.

Enamel paint
Clean with a solution of 1 gal lukewarm water and 1 tsp washing soda. If the walls are stained or mildewed, add ½ c chlorine bleach to the solution. Do not use ammonia or all-purpose cleaners containing ammonia—they can dull and etch the paint.

Special problems
You may have to wash the entire wall thoroughly after treating stains.
Fingerprints and non-greasy stains: Sponge with a solution of ½ gal lukewarm water and ¼ c washing soda *or* TSP, *or* an all-purpose cleaner without ammonia. Then rinse off with a damp sponge.
Greasy stains: Using a cloth dipped in alcohol, rub from the center of the stain out. Use a dry cloth to blot as you go. Rub lightly and blot until stain is gone.

Your home's walls collect almost as much dust and oil as your furniture and floors. Dust and vacuum them regularly, and clean overall once a year.

Holes and gouges: Scrape off any loose paint with a putty knife. Fill the hole or gouge with spackle, and allow to dry. Then sand it smooth, and touch up with matching paint.
Flaking paint: Soften the paint with a solution of ½ gal hot water and ¼ c TSP. Let it dry, then brush or sand it smooth, and repaint.
Preparing to repaint: Sponge with a solution of 1 gal hot water and ½ c TSP, then rinse. Allow the walls to dry thoroughly before repainting. If you have had mildew problems, add a commercial mildewcide (available at paint stores) to your primer or paint. If the paint was applied with a roller, also touch it up with a roller—a brush will not give the same texture.

Flat paint
Clean with a solution of 1 gal lukewarm water and 2 tbsp washing soda *or* TSP. Rinse with plain water. Overlap the sections to avoid streaks. Use only white cloths—colored sponges may leave a dye on the walls. Keep your cleaning solution and rinse water clean, or you will only be moving the dirt around more evenly. Don't scrub—it will burnish the paint and leave shiny spots. If the walls are especially grimy, it may be easier to clean them as much as possible, then repaint.

Special problems
Test stain-removing solutions on an inconspicuous spot before using—many all-purpose cleaners and stain-removing products are too strong for flat paint.
Fingerprints and non-greasy stains: Sponge with a solution of ½ gal lukewarm water and 1 tbsp TSP *or* 1 tsp liquid detergent, then rinse.
Greasy stains: Blot with a crumpled paper towel. Hold

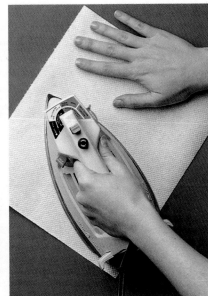

To remove greasy stains from non-washable wall coverings: **1.** Blot with crumpled paper towel until any liquid is absorbed.

2. Hold several paper towels over the spot, and press with a warm iron, changing the towels as they absorb the stain.

3. Apply a wall-cleaning paste (see box below), let it dry, brush it off, then blot with a solvent-based cleaning fluid.

two or three clean pieces of paper towel over the spot, and press with a warm iron. Repeat until stain is almost gone, changing the paper each time. Then blot with a commercial or homemade wall-cleaning paste (see box to right).

Holes and gouges: Same as for enamel paint.

Flaking paint: Same as for enamel paint.

Preparing to repaint: Same as for enamel paint.

Washable wallpaper

Use a solution of 1 gal warm water and ¼ c washing soda *or* TSP. Avoid saturating the paper, especially the seams. Then rinse with a sponge dipped in plain water and wrung almost dry.

Special problems

To repair torn or blistered paper, see Ortho's book, *Basic Home Repairs*.

Fingerprints, tape marks, and non-greasy stains: Rub with an art-gum eraser. If some of the color or pattern rubs off, retouch it with colored pencils (dull finish) or acrylic paints (shiny finish). If the stain remains, apply a commercial or homemade wall-cleaning paste, then wash with your usual cleaning solution.

Greasy stains: Blot with crumpled paper towels. Hold several clean towels over the spot, and press with a warm iron. Repeat until the grease is absorbed, changing the paper each time. If the stain remains, use a commercial or homemade wall-cleaning paste, then wash with your usual cleaning solution.

Mildew: Spray lightly with a commercial mildew remover, *or* sponge with a cloth dampened in alcohol. Rub off any remaining gray stains with an art-gum eraser or wall-cleaning paste.

Non-washable wallpaper

Non-washable wallpaper must be cleaned with a solvent because it is vulnerable to water. Dampen several terrycloth towels with kerosene. Allow them to air dry. Wrap one of the towels around the head of a broom or mop, securing it with tape or rubber bands. Wipe the walls from the ceiling down, overlapping the strips as you move around the room. Turn or change the cloths as they become grimy.

Fabric

Because unbacked fabric coverings would be difficult to clean in place, they usually can be removed for washing or dry cleaning. They also may be stapled to the wall, or to wood strips or frames. Unless you know how to remove and clean unbacked fabric coverings, you may want to have a professional do it. Consult a wallpaper hanger to locate a fabric cleaner in your area. After fabrics have been cleaned, protect them by spraying with a water and soil repellent. Silk coverings should always be cleaned professionally.

Special problems

Same as for washable wallpaper.

Homemade wall-cleaning paste

Mix fuller's earth (for dark surfaces), *or* cornstarch *or* whiting (for light surfaces) with a cleaning fluid. Apply the paste to the stain and let it dry thoroughly. Brush it into a dustpan. Then treat any remaining spot with the cleaning solution mentioned for the specific type of walls or wall covering.

Wood paneling

Wood paneling, like wood furniture, is either lacquered or coated with plastic, or oiled. An oiled surface has a soft sheen and feels oiled—lacquer and plastic generally are shinier, and may be waxed.

Oiled

Clean by wiping with boiled linseed oil or lemon oil (light finishes) or Danish oil (darker finishes). Remove any excess to avoid leaving a dust-attracting film. Do not use furniture polishes containing silicone, which eventually will break down the finish. Spot clean and dust with lemon oil on a cloth between overall cleanings.

Lacquered, plastic-coated, and/or waxed

Clean waxed paneling by rubbing it with a beeswax- or carnauba-based paste wax. The wax will hide most small scratches and marks, and even out the finish. Follow label directions. If the paneling is lacquered or covered with a plastic coating, clean it with warm, soapy water, then wax it if desired.

Special problems

If the problem has penetrated into the wood itself, it will be difficult to repair. You may have to refinish or replace an entire panel to get the wall to look good again. Whenever you buy new wood paneling, be sure to buy an extra replacement panel in case any part of the wall is irreparably damaged.

Stains on lacquered, waxed, or plastic-coated paneling: Rub with your usual wax or with warm, soapy water. If stain remains, use a commercial furniture-restorer product (available at home-improvement centers), following label instructions.

Stains on oiled wood: Rub gently with lemon oil, using fine steel wool. Reoil, then wipe off excess.

Moisture damage: Damp, puffy sections of paneling indicate moisture damage. Seepage and condensation will cause the paneling to pop away from the wall, to warp, and eventually to rot. Look for rusty nails, and check the wall and insulation behind the paneling for dampness. For details on moisture problems, see pages 74–75.

Tape and stickers: Place a cloth saturated with your usual cleaning solution, wax, or oil onto the spot where the tape or sticker is. Tape it in place with Holland tape. Leave the cloth on overnight, then remove it and scrub off the tape or stickers.

Scratches and holes: You can hide small scratches with your usual wax or oil. If that doesn't work, use a commercial wood-putty stick (available at home-improvement centers), matching the color of your paneling. Follow label directions.

Insect damage: Check your paneling occasionally for signs of insects. Look for soft, hollow areas and small entrance holes, especially near the floor. If you suspect an infestation, call a professional exterminator for help—the pests are likely to be in the walls behind the paneling and even in your furniture. To help identify which insect you might be dealing with and how to eliminate, see Pests, pages 66–69.

Cork tiles

Because cork is not naturally washable, it generally is coated with a sealer to make it moisture resistant. Dust cork frequently. Wipe with a cloth dipped in a mild solution of detergent and water, and wrung almost dry. Rinse with a cloth dipped in plain water.

Special problems

To repair and replace damaged tiles, see Ortho's book, *Basic Home Repairs.*

Stains: Blot up as much of the staining material as possible. Apply a commercial or homemade wall-cleaning paste to the stain, and let it dry. Brush it into a dustpan and vacuum off any of the remaining compound.

Ceramic tiles and plastics

Wash with an all-purpose cleaner, commercial cleaning foam, disinfectant cleaner, or a solution of 1 gal warm water and ½ c ammonia. Rinse well. Avoid soaps—they can leave a white film. Scrub the grout between ceramic tiles with scouring powder, or a commercial grout cleaner and a grout brush.

Special problems

To repair and replace damaged tiles, see Ortho's book, *Basic Home Repairs.*

Chips, cracks, and small holes: Wash, rinse, and allow to dry. Then fill cracks, holes, and chips with silicone caulking. With your fingers, wipe off the excess—caulking is hard to remove once it has set.

Soap and mineral deposits: Scrub with a solution of ½ gal warm water and ¼ c ammonia, then rinse.

Plaster walls

Clean according to the type of paint used.

For overall cleaning of non-washable and fabric wall coverings, wring out towels in kerosene, air-dry them, wrap around a broom head, then wipe from ceiling down.

Special problems

To repair damaged plaster, see Ortho's book, *Basic Home Repairs.*

Older plaster walls may have "hot spots" that appear as dark patches when wallpaper glue or flat paint is applied. These spots are caused by excess alkalis in the plaster. Neutralize them by sponging with equal parts vinegar and water. If, by the time this solution has dried, the spot hasn't faded, apply the solution a second time.

Ceilings

Whenever possible, ask your home-improvement center dealer for guidelines on the techniques and products suitable for your particular ceiling material.

Routine care

Ceilings need only minimal routine care—remove the cobwebs and dust occasionally. Use a lamb's-wool duster with an extension handle, a cloth-wrapped broom, or the brush attachment of your vacuum.

Periodic care

For overall cleaning, use the same solution as for walls, depending on what the ceiling is made of. Some suspended ceilings can be removed panel by panel for cleaning. A dry sponge (available at some janitorial-supply houses and home-improvement centers) is especially useful for cleaning ceilings.

Special problems

The most common ceiling problem is water damage from leaks. Water will stain acoustical ceilings and wood, and cause latex ceilings to warp. After repairing the leak, let the ceiling dry out thoroughly before repainting or repairing. Then proceed as outlined below. Ceiling repairs are outlined in Ortho's book, *Basic Home Repairs.*

Acoustical: Because they have an open texture or holes and are porous, these ceilings cannot be scrubbed. Repaint with a non-abridging paint—one that doesn't seal off the acoustical properties of the material (available at paint stores).

Latex tile: Some of these tiles or suspended ceiling panels can be scrubbed. Remove dirty panels, if possible, and clean them and washable tiles with an all-purpose cleaning solution *or* a solution of 1 gal water and ¼ c TSP. Lay warped panels face-down on a flat surface after cleaning, and weight them down with furniture or bricks until they are dry. If the tile is stapled or glued to the ceiling, and has cupped or warped, restaple or glue only after the underceiling and the tile are thoroughly dry.

Sprayed acoustical ceilings: These ceilings can be cleaned by professionals using a water-spray technique. However, it's usually easier and cheaper to repaint them. Use a non-abridging paint—one that doesn't seal off the acoustical properties of the material (available at paint stores).

Wood: If your wood ceiling is stained from leaks, you may have to paint it or apply a darker-colored wood stain. Before painting, brush white shellac over any knots to prevent the resins from bleeding through the paint.

For routine cleaning of beamed and sloping ceilings, attach an extension handle to a lamb's wool duster and remove dust and cobwebs. Clean overall once a year.

DOORS

Because doors are constantly being opened and closed, they take more battering than most other structural parts of your house. See Ortho's book, *Basic Home Repairs*, for loose hinges, warped doors, loose door jambs, and cracked thresholds. This section discusses how to clean and repair doors, doorknobs, locks, and sliding doors.

Routine care
Spot-clean fingerprints around doorknobs and jambs.

Periodic care and special problems
Clean your doors overall whenever you wash your windows. See Woodwork to clean specific finishes. The following copy deals with doorknobs, locks, and sliding doors.

Brass doorknobs: Polish with brass polish. So that the polish doesn't mark the paint or wood surrounding the knob and strike plate, protect it with masking tape or a cardboard shield cut to fit.

Other metal doorknobs: Most metal hardware other than brass is covered with a protective coat of lacquer. This lacquer may eventually wear off and look spotty. Remove the doorknob. Wipe it off with lacquer thinner, *or* soak it in boiling water for a few minutes, then peel it off. Next, coat or dip the knob in clear lacquer. Let it dry thoroughly before replacing. Protect the knob further by coating with a paste wax, and buffing.

Glass doorknobs: Wipe with hot, soapy water. If the glass begins to look cloudy, remove the knob and soak it in hot, soapy water with a little ammonia added. Rinse well, and allow to dry thoroughly before replacing.

Porcelain doorknobs: Wipe with hot, soapy water. To remove stains and restore the shine, rub with a paste of water and baking soda *or* washing soda, then rinse. When it's dry, coat the knob with paste wax, and buff.

Locks: To lubricate locks, use powdered graphite (oil attracts dirt) two or three times a year, especially during cold weather (when they are most likely to stick or freeze). If the lock sticks in spite of lubrication, it probably is clogged with accumulated dirt and grease, and will require a thorough cleaning. Disassemble it carefully, remembering each step so that you can put it back together properly. Clean all parts with alcohol, using a toothbrush. Reassemble, and lubricate with powdered graphite. For more detailed information on locks, see Ortho's book, *Basic Home Repairs*.

Sliding glass doors: If the doors don't slide smoothly, vacuum the bottom tracks and scrape out any dirt, wax, or paint. Then wipe the tracks with fine steel wool, and lubricate them with powdered graphite or silicone lubricant. If they still won't slide smoothly, check for bent rails at the top or bottom. Use a block of wood and a hammer to straighten them.

Sliding wooden doors: Sliding closet doors have a roller mechanism on top, which fits into a rail, and a bottom track to keep them from swinging in or out. The roller mechanism has a dial or screw for adjusting the height of the door. If the doors aren't sliding smoothly, check that the roller is in the rail, and that the rail is not bent. If necessary, adjust the mechanism up or down.

WOODWORK

Routine care
Spot-clean painted woodwork with an all-purpose cleaner without ammonia—ammonia can dull painted surfaces. If your woodwork is oiled instead of painted, clean and reoil with boiled linseed *or* lemon oil.

Periodic care and special problems
Use the same cleaner mentioned under routine care to clean painted or oiled woodwork. A good time for overall cleaning of your woodwork is when you clean your walls and ceilings.

Chipped paint: Scrape off the loose paint, then scrub with a solution of ½ gal hot water and ¼ c TSP, *or* sand smooth and repaint. The paint may be chipping off because of excess moisture. Check the windows and doors nearby for sufficient weatherstripping and proper ventilation.

Holes and gouges: Scrape away loose paint. Fill the hole or gouge with spackling compound. When spackle is dry, sand it smooth with sandpaper, and touch up with paint *or* reoil. Use wood putty for oiled surfaces.

Stains on painted woodwork: Most woodwork is painted with enamel paint because it forms a harder, easier-to-clean surface than flat paint. Try removing stains with homemade or commercial wall-cleaning paste (see page 29). Leave it on until dry—half an hour or more—then brush it off into a dustpan. Or try undiluted all-purpose cleaner without ammonia. When the stain is gone, rinse well and rub gently with alcohol, lacquer thinner, *or* lemon oil to restore the shine.

Stains on oiled woodwork: Clean stains with lemon oil, using fine steel wool.

Clean unpainted woodwork with boiled linseed oil or lemon oil. Rub stains with lemon oil and fine steel wool.

WINDOWS

Routine care

Dust *or* wipe the frames, sills, and bars whenever you dust and vacuum. Regular dusting will help keep the glass clean.

Periodic care and special problems

Wash glass as frequently as necessary (see page 79). Check glass for cracks; check weatherstripping for damage. See the following for cleaning specific types of window frames and special problems.

Casement windows: Clean and lubricate the rods used for wooden windows. Metal frame windows usually open with a crank mechanism. This may jam occasionally, possibly because of dirt and grime accumulating inside the mechanism on the gears. Remove the crank and clean the gears with alcohol, using a toothbrush. Then apply fresh grease (available at hardware stores). If the gears are worn, replace the whole mechanism. Large hardware stores or lumberyards that sell casement windows can order some for you if they don't have them in stock. Take the old crank with you so the replacement will match exactly. To replace glass, see Ortho's book, *Basic Home Repairs.*

Double-hung windows: Occasionally the channels on either side of the frame become sticky with dirt or paint. Scrape them clean with a small chisel or knife, then lubricate with candle wax, paraffin, *or* silicone lubricant. For more details, see Ortho's book, *Basic Home Repairs.*

Sliding windows: These require virtually no maintenance, as long as the channel in which they slide is kept clean. For more on sliding glass doors, see page 32.

Inside window screens: The screens on windows that open out often attach to inside fasteners. When painting, don't get paint on these fasteners—it can make them immovable. If the fasteners are already painted, remove the paint—either with a commercial paint remover or by scraping it off. Clean the screens once a year by removing them and scrubbing them outdoors with a wire brush and a garden hose.

Condensation: When warm, moist air from inside hits cold glass, the moisture condenses into drops that run down the inside of the window. Limit the problem by insulating with storm windows; eliminate some of the moisture inside by using a dehumidifier and improving your ventilation. If condensation is a serious problem in cold weather, it may mean that all the wood in the structure of your house is damp with condensation, which can cause such problems as wood rot, peeling paint, and the eventual deterioration of the structure. Check the insulation in your house, and make certain you have vapor barriers on the warm side of rooms. You may be able to see the insulation by unscrewing an electrical outlet.

Drafts: If you have drafts, you probably need weatherstripping. For information on caulking windows and installing weatherstripping, see Ortho's book, *Energy-Saving Projects for the Home.*

Paint drips: To scrape paint off smooth glass, use a razorblade scraper. To remove paint from textured windows, brush windows with a water-based paint-removing gel, leave on for a few minutes, then wipe off. Wear rubber

To help keep windows clean, routinely dust or wipe frames and sills. For window-washing techniques, see page 79.

gloves to protect your hands, and don't drip the remover onto sashes and sills.

Rattles: There are several reasons why windows may rattle: **1.** The glass itself may not be securely puttied into the frame. To correct, add an additional bead of window putty to the outside frame while pushing on the glass. **2.** The sash may be too loose in the frame. To correct, add ¼-inch strips of hardwood or felt weatherstripping to both sides of the inner sash. **3.** There may be a gap in the top rail. To correct, add felt weatherstripping between the top and bottom frames. **4.** If metal casement windows rattle, you may need to tighten the crank mechanism or shim the latch. See Ortho's book, *Basic Home Repairs,* for detailed instructions.

Rusty metal: Deal with rust problems quickly—if you don't, the rust will continue to corrode the frames, which you will have to replace eventually. Arrest the rust with a commercial rust remover/retardant paint. If necessary, sand the frames with sandpaper or steel wool, paint with a rust-retardant primer or kerosene, and then repaint.

To clean windows as professionals do, see page 79.

WOOD FURNITURE

Wood furniture is either waxed, oiled, or coated with a plastic finish. Check the hang-tag for manufacturer's care recommendations. Check the box on page 35 to determine which protective finish can be used for your furniture. To protect wood further, try not to place it in direct sunlight. This can cause it to crack and can lighten the finish. Also avoid heat sources, windows, and doors. Temperature extremes can affect the wood and the finish. Use felt pads under lamp bases and other objects you place on furniture. *Or* cover table tops with a sheet of shatter-resistant glass. Use trivets under hot serving bowls on your dining room table to prevent heat marks, and use coasters under beverages to prevent water and alcohol stains. (To remove such stains, see Periodic care and special problems, below.)

Routine care

Dust regularly with a dry, lintless cloth such as cheesecloth, undershirts, and flannel. Chemically treated cloths also are good, but some contain oil. Use these for oiled and plastic-coated wood, but not for woods protected by wax. You can damp-dust furniture with a damp cloth or sponge to remove the grime. Then dry thoroughly, and rewax or reoil. Wood should have as little contact with water as possible, since water can raise its grain. If you use paste wax, you can buff between waxings occasionally to bring out the shine. Clean laminated plastic or plastic-coated furniture with an all-purpose cleaner and a damp sponge. Avoid abrasive scouring pads and powders.

Periodic care and special problems

Wax or polish as needed, following manufacturer's directions. Aerosols, oils, and liquid polishes usually are flammable—they should be used sparingly, and in a well-ventilated room. Wash or discard the cloth so that it doesn't become a fire hazard. Apply thin coats of paste wax with a cloth, using a circular motion. When dry, buff with a soft, lintless cloth. For a higher gloss, apply a second coat and buff again. Pour liquid waxes directly on the piece of furniture or on a soft, lintless cloth. Rub polish into the furniture. Buff lightly with a dry cloth to bring out the shine.

Alcohol spills: Rub with spirits of camphor (available from a pharmacy), *or* toothpaste, *or* boiled linseed oil. Wipe off the excess, and polish or wax as usual.

Bubbles in veneered surfaces: Using a sharp razor blade, cut into the bubble, following the wood grain. Soften the veneer by placing a wet cloth on the surface and pressing gently with a warm iron. Lift the edges with a dull knife, and apply yellow carpenter's glue to the underside with an artist's brush. Smooth the edges down with a rolling pin, then clamp or weight down overnight until set. Remove excess glue with hot water.

Cigarette burns: If the burn is superficial, rub with linseed oil, *or* olive oil, *or* petroleum jelly. Treat deeper burns as gouges.

Dents: Place a damp cloth over the dent, and iron with a warm steam iron until the grain rises into place. Be very careful to go slowly, and check to make certain the steam is not damaging the finish.

Protect wood furniture with a coat of wax, polish, or plastic finish. Tabletops and chair arms may need more frequent waxing than other furniture parts. For special problems such as stains or scratches, see text on this page.

Gouges: If the gouge is on a flat surface, remove the wax or polish and some of the finish with deodorized mineral spirits and fine steel wool. The whole area will have to be refinished to look even. Fill the gouge with a commercial wood putty that matches the color of the wood. When dry, sand smooth, refinish, and rewax.

Ink: On light wood, rub with a paste of lemon juice and salt. Rinse, and polish as usual. As it is very difficult to remove liquid ink that has penetrated into the grain, you might have to refinish the piece.

Lifting edges on veneered surfaces: Repair as for bubbles, being certain to remove as much dry glue as possible from underneath.

Loose joints: Tighten all screws and bolts in loose bed rails, tables, and chairs. Too much wobble in a piece of furniture can mean that a supporting part is not properly carrying its own weight and is thus putting other parts under undue stress. This can lead to serious repair problems. To disassemble the piece, first remove any corner braces. If possible, twist dowels, or pull on mortise and tenon joints to separate the parts. Do not take apart any more joints than necessary—you could weaken those that are still strong. Lightly sand the old glue out of the socket and dowel or tenon, and apply white glue to both pieces. Push together, and clamp overnight to dry. Wipe off the excess glue with warm water. For more extensive repairs, consult a professional.

Scratches: To cover superficial scratches that have not penetrated the finish, use your regular wax or oil. If scratches still are noticeable, use a commercial scratch hider or crayon (available at hardware stores) that matches the color of your finish.

Stains: First determine whether the stain is in the wax finish or the polish, or in the varnish or shellac, or whether it has penetrated the wood itself. After removing any of the staining matter or solid material, try rubbing the stain with your usual wax, oil, or polish. If the stain still remains, apply the wax, oil, or polish with fine steel wool. Then rub the stain as follows: Put olive oil on the stain, and add enough rottenstone powder (a mild abrasive available at pharmacies) to make a paste. Rub in the direction of the wood grain with a soft cloth. If the stain still remains, it is probably in the wood itself. In that case, it will have to be bleached *or* sanded and refinished. You may want to have this done professionally.

Sticking table-extension mechanism: Open the table to its full extension. Scrape out any accumulated food particles, and chisel away dirt and grime with a putty knife. Spray the whole mechanism, whether wooden or metal, with a commercial silicone spray *or* powdered graphite so that it will slide more easily.

Water marks: Rub with linseed oil, *or* olive oil, *or* petroleum jelly until the white mark disappears. If marks are extensive, strip off the polish or wax by applying alcohol (unless it is a shellac finish) *or* turpentine (unless it is a varnish finish), and then quickly remove the stain with your regular wax or polish. Rewax.

Protective products for wood furniture

Paste wax: Paste waxes contain either carnauba wax, beeswax, or paraffin (see label for use on light or dark woods). Apply sparingly, and buff with a soft cloth to bring up the shine. Clean with lukewarm water, and buff often. Rewax only when buffing no longer brings out the shine.

Liquid or aerosol furniture polishes: Some furniture polishes are shinier than others—experiment to find the one you prefer. They contain varying amounts of wax or acrylic resins, water, and/or solvents. Most are used to both clean and protect. Apply sparingly—never use so much that the wax or resins form a dull film that can't be buffed. Apply the polish only when the finish begins to dull, or when you're cleaning the furniture—not every time you dust it. Avoid polishes containing silicone, which eventually will deteriorate the finish. Observe the precautions on the label.

Oils: Do not use any oils on waxed wood—oil dissolves wax. Lemon oils effectively clean and shine most oiled furniture, and furniture that hasn't been polished with acrylic polishes. Lemon oil is poisonous, and children may be attracted to it because of its pleasant odor—so keep in a locked cabinet. Both boiled linseed oil and Danish oil (linseed oil with a color stain added for use on darker wood) are used occasionally to clean and polish oiled wood. Linseed oils are highly flammable and poisonous. Keep away from children, and do not store for any length of time—they may ignite spontaneously.

Dusting sprays: These are designed to attract dust to your dusting cloth.

Wickerwork, cane, and bamboo furniture

Furniture made of twigs or rods is usually protected against stains, loose joints, and warping with a coat of paint, shellac, or varnish. If the finish has been worn or washed off, it should be reapplied after a thorough cleaning. Protect against heat sources and extreme fluctuations in humidity and temperature.

Routine care

Dust regularly with a soft brush dampened with furniture oil *or* water. If the furniture is flat, use a sponge. *Or* use the brush and crevice attachments of your vacuum cleaner.

Periodic care

Rattan, cane, and bamboo: Moisten once a year with a fine spray to keep the fibers from drying out, shrinking, or stretching. Dry in the sun if possible. For a thorough cleaning, and before applying a protective finish, scrub the furniture (outdoors, or indoors in the bathtub) with warm, soapy water. To keep light-colored furniture from changing color and to prevent stickiness, add 1 tbsp salt to each quart of solution. Rinse well with water, and dry near an open window (preferably in the sun), or in a warm room with a fan. Refinish, if necessary. Wax, if desired, with a natural-base wax to protect it further.

Reed, rush, and seagrass: Wipe with a solution of mild detergent and water on a sponge. Wring out as much of the solution as possible—the fibers should not get too wet. Rinse with a sponge wrung in plain water, and allow to air. Spray with a protective coat of varnish, shellac, or paint.

Special problems

Some furniture repair shops are equipped to handle major repairs on wicker, cane, and bamboo furniture.

Mildew: Using a soft paint brush, paint light-colored and painted furniture with a solution of chlorine bleach and warm water. *Or* spray with a chemical mildew remover. Rub darker wicker, cane, and rush with diluted ammonia on a soft cloth. Rinse well, and dry thoroughly—in the sun, if possible. To prevent mildew, coat with two layers of shellac.

Yellowing: Sponge with a solution of equal parts water and lemon juice *or* vinegar. Rinse, and dry in the sun.

Cracked finish: Scrub with a solution of ¼ c TSP and 1 gal warm water, using a stiff brush. Rinse well, and dry. Then refinish with shellac.

Sagging seat: Wash with very hot water, and dry in the sun.

Unraveling: Soak ends in warm water until they are pliable. Brush with wood glue, and push back into place. Secure with a small nail or brad until glue is dry. Spot refinish if necessary. If a piece is broken off, you may be able to find a replacement cane in a hardware store or hobby shop. Soak the new piece until it is pliable, then wrap or weave it into place. Brush the ends with wood glue and push them into place. Secure with a small nail or brad until glue is dry.

Any fabric can be used to upholster or slipcover a piece of furniture, as long as it is sturdy enough to resist friction and is able to be cleaned or laundered. Before cleaning upholstery fabric, refer to the hang-tag for instructions. If you do not have the tag, determine the fabric content as closely as possible, and use the chart on page 37 for cleaning agents and methods. It is also important to consider the texture of the fabric. For example, vacuum velvets, brocades, and nubby yarns frequently to avoid dirt build-up that eventually can make them impossible to clean. You can use a vacuum or soft upholstery brush on other fabrics, but only if the brush is kept very clean. Otherwise you will simply be brushing the dirt and oils into the fabric. Most fabrics are protected with an anti-static product that also helps them resist spots and stains. Wool is almost always treated by the manufacturer to repel insects. However, because these protective treatments wash off when a spot is removed or the fabric is cleaned overall, they must be reapplied. Replace the original protection by means of any of several commercially available sprays.

Routine care

Vacuum upholstery with the upholstery-brush attachment. Use the flat nozzle to reach into crevices and around cording. Or soften a natural bristle brush in boiling water, shake out the excess water, and brush the fabric in the direction of the nap. When vacuuming, go over each section five or six times with slow, back-and-forth strokes. Do not vacuum down-filled furniture—the suction will pull the feathers through the fabric.

Periodic care and special problems

Deep clean when the fabric looks dull, or when stain removal has left streaks of clean areas next to dull areas. You may want to have your upholstery cleaned professionally. This generally gives good results and takes less of your time, but may be expensive. To do your own deep cleaning, use a commercial upholstery shampoo, or make your own cleaning foam (see recipe on this page). Pretreat spots. Test both spot removers and cleaners on an inconspicuous area to determine whether the color will run or fade. Because washable fabrics have a tendency to shrink, you may have better results cleaning the cushions or slipcovers in place, or having the furniture cleaned professionally.

To deep clean: Scrub commercial or homemade foam into the fabric, using a soft cloth or natural bristle brush softened in boiling water. Overlap each area to avoid streaks. Rinse with a damp cloth, and wipe dry with a terrycloth towel. Finish drying in front of a fan or an open window. Do not overwet. When the fabric is dry, spray with a commercial anti-static spray to replace the finish.

To remove stains: See pages 42–51. The most common stains on upholstery are from body and hair oils on the arms and headrests. These stains must be removed with a grease solvent, such as dry-cleaning fluid, before overall cleaning. Newspaper ink is also a common problem; try to avoid placing newspapers on the furniture.

To clean slipcovers: Dry clean or hand wash in cold-

Vacuum upholstery regularly, going over each section five or six times. Deep-clean when the fabric looks dull, but avoid overwetting. See text for instructions.

water soap or mild detergent, and line dry (the heat from washers and dryers can cause fabrics and cording to shrink). Do not wash textured, plush, or pile fabrics. If the room is warm enough to dry them in a few hours, replace laundered slipcovers while they are still slightly damp. There will be less shrinkage if they dry in their natural shape. Touch up with a warm iron. Zippered cushion covers on upholstered furniture are not slipcovers. Do not remove them. The zippers in cushions are for the upholsterer's convenience only.

Homemade upholstery shampoo

Mix 2 tbsp soap flakes, 2 tbsp ammonia or washing soda, and 1 qt hot water. Let the mixture sit until jelled. Whip with a hand mixer or in the blender. Use the foam only to clean. Avoid overwetting the fabric.

Manufacturer's cleaning codes

W Use only water-mixed cleaning agents, such as soap flakes or mild detergents.

S Use only solvent-based cleaning products, such as commercial dry-cleaning liquids, and pastes containing no water.

WS Use either water- or solvent-based agents.

X Do not use liquid cleaning agents of any type. Clean only by vacuuming or brushing lightly to remove soil. Consult a professional for deep cleaning and stain removal.

Cleaning upholstery fabrics

Cotton, synthetic, and linen	Use a commercial or homemade upholstery shampoo, *or* have fabrics cleaned professionally. After deep cleaning, treat with a commercial anti-static spray. To remove stains, see pages 42–51.
Silk	Have cleaned professionally.
Leather	Leather may crack if exposed to temperature extremes or sunlight. Do not place near radiators or windows. Wipe with a damp sponge dipped in saddle soap *or* mild soap suds. Wipe off excess, and polish with a soft, dry cloth. To keep leather from cracking, condition with commercial leather conditioner or neat's foot oil. Most oils and conditioners will darken leather. Use white petroleum jelly on white or light leather. Do not use waxes or mineral oil—they damage the finish. To remove stains, see pages 42–51.
Moire	Have cleaned professionally. The pattern is created by water marks—any liquid will damage it.
Vinyl	Clean with a solution of mild dishwashing liquid and warm water on a sponge. Rinse with a damp sponge. To prevent hardening and cracking, polish once a year with a creamy furniture polish after cleaning. Do not use solvents, abrasives, leather conditioners, or strong household cleaners to clean or to remove stains. Avoid acetone.
Velvet, velour, wool, olefin, and corduroy	Have cleaned professionally. Remove stains with dry-cleaning fluid on a soft cloth. Test on an inconspicuous area first.

FABRIC CARE

It is always advisable to keep the labels and tags accompanying clothing and fabrics for specific care instructions from the manufacturer. If you no longer have these instructions, take the clothing or a swatch to a professional cleaner for identification. If you don't find the name of the fabric in the chart below, it may be a trade name. Arnel, for example, is a triacetate; Lycra and Qiana are nylons. To remove stains from fabrics, see the Stain Chart, pages 42–51.

Laundry

To get the best results with your wash, follow these suggestions:

1. Keep labels and manufacturer's instructions filed in your desk for quick reference. Or see the guidelines in the chart below for washing or dry cleaning fabrics.

2. Before loading laundry and machine, empty pockets and close zippers, snaps, and hooks. This will prevent damage to your laundry and to your washer and dryer.

3. Repair tears and holes before laundering fabrics, otherwise the action of the machine or hand washing may damage the fabric further.

Test washable fabric for colorfastness on an inside seam. Rub some soapy water on the seam, then rub with a white cloth. If the cloth is stained by the dye, set the color by washing the fabric in the hottest water possible, adding ½ c vinegar to the final rinse.

Fabric	To clean and press	Cautions and comments
Acetate	Dry clean *or* hand wash with warm water and mild detergent. May use oxygen bleach. Drip dry. Press on the wrong side with iron set on low heat.	Do not soak. Avoid acetone and amyl acetate, strong alkalis such as washing soda, and chlorine bleach. May water spot, shrink, or stretch.
Acrylic	Hand *or* machine wash (gentle cycle) with warm water and detergent. Use fabric softener occasionally. Dry clean pile fabrics. May use oxygen bleach. Drip dry *or* tumble dry on low heat. Press with warm steam iron.	Do not wring. Acrylic is susceptible to static cling. May pill.
Angora	*See* Wool.	
Batiste	A type of weave—*see* Cotton, Synthetic, or Wool.	
Boucle	A type of weave—*see* Cotton, Synthetic, or Wool.	Do not wring or stretch.
Broadcloth	A type of weave—*see* Cotton or Wool.	
Brocade	A type of weave—*see* Cotton, Silk, Synthetic, or Wool.	Avoid abrasion.
Burlap (jute)	Hand wash in cool water with mild detergent. Air-dry flat. Press with warm steam iron.	Do not wring or twist.
Camel hair	*See* Wool.	
Canvas	A type of weave, usually cotton. Wipe with warm, soapy water, then rinse with a damp sponge. Air dry. Press with warm steam iron.	Do not overwet.
Cashmere	*See* Wool.	
Challis	A type of weave—*see* Cotton, Synthetic, or Wool.	
Chamois	Natural or synthetic leather. Machine wash (gentle cycle) with warm water and detergent. Air-dry stretched flat. Do not iron. Knead with your hands to soften.	Avoid bleaches. If chamois stiffens, soak in warm water and olive oil.

4. Wash and dry starched, non-colorfast, or linty items separately from other loads.

5. Treat heavily soiled and stained fabrics before washing them. Generally, you can safely apply a paste of your usual detergent and water to the stain. Greasy stains respond well to a solvent or detergent (depending on the specific fabric); blood, milk, and egg stains usually can be removed with an enzyme product *or* washing soda. See the Stain Chart on pages 42–51.

6. Before using stain removers, first test them on an inconspicuous area of the fabric, such as an inside seam.

7. Dissolve bleaches, detergent, water conditioners, and powdered stain-removing products in the wash water before adding the dry laundry. Undissolved powders and unmixed liquids can spot fabrics.

8. Leave plenty of room for agitation in the washer—this action is what cleans the laundry.

9. Don't overload the dryer—laundry needs plenty of room to dry evenly and without wrinkles.

10. To prevent wrinkles, remove and shake clothes as soon as you remove them from the dryer.

11. Clean washer and dryer lint traps after every load.

The quickest and safest way to treat stains on washable fabrics is to rinse them in cool water, spray the stain with a pre-wash product, and then wash; *or* apply a paste of your usual detergent and water. Leave the paste on for half an hour, then wash as usual.

Fabric	To clean and press	Cautions and comments
Chenille	A type of weave—*see* Cotton or Synthetic.	
Chiffon	A type of weave—may be silk or synthetic. Dry clean or hand wash in warm water and mild detergent. Tumble dry on low heat, *or* air-dry flat. Press with warm steam iron.	Do not wring or twist. Avoid bleaches.
Chintz	Glazed cotton—*see* Cotton.	
Corduroy	A type of weave—may be cotton or synthetic. Dry clean, *or* machine wash with warm water and detergent. May use oxygen bleach. Tumble dry on medium heat. Press on the wrong side with warm steam iron.	May shrink—be certain to check the label when you buy corduroy clothing. Some clothing must be dry cleaned.
Cotton	If cotton has been pre-shrunk, machine wash with hot water and detergent. If you can't tell, hand wash cotton with lukewarm water and cold-water soap. May use chlorine or oxygen bleach. Tumble dry on medium to high heat, *or* air dry. Press with hot steam iron; *or* press with warm to hot iron while fabric is still damp.	To check colored fabrics for colorfastness before washing, wet an inside seam and rub it with a white cloth. If color runs, wash fabric separately, adding 1 c vinegar to the final rinse to set the dye.
Dacron	Trade name for a polyester. Machine wash (gentle cycle) using warm water and detergent. May use oxygen bleach. Tumble dry on low heat, removing promptly to avoid wrinkles. Press on the wrong side with warm steam iron.	Avoid extreme temperature changes; avoid heat. Avoid acetone and amyl acetate. Do not soak in strong alkalis such as washing soda, or use chlorine bleaches. May pill.
Fake fur	Follow label for care recommendations.	
Felt	A type of weave—may be wool, fur, and/or hair. Dry clean. Press on the wrong side with warm steam iron.	Avoid water, bleaches, and abrasion. Tears and stains easily.
Fur	Dry clean. Do not iron.	Susceptible to insect damage—protect with moth balls or crystals.
Glass cloth	Wash in machine (gentle cycle) with hot water and detergent, *or* wash by hand, but wear rubber gloves to avoid glass slivers. Hang to drip dry. Do not iron.	Do not scrub or wring. May tear.

FABRIC CARE

Fabric	To clean and press	Cautions and comments
Lace	A type of weave—may be cotton or synthetic. Hand wash with cool water and cold-water soap. Tumble dry with no heat, *or* air-dry stretched flat. Press with steam iron on low heat.	Do not wring or twist. May stretch or tear.
Lawn	*See* Organdy.	
Leather	Dry clean *or* wipe with a leather conditioner or soap foam, then wipe dry. Do not iron. Wipe mildew with alcohol.	Avoid water and bleaches. Susceptible to mildew—use a commercial mildew product made especially for leather (available at shoe repair shops). For more information on leather, see the section on Upholstery, pages 36–37.
Linen	If linen has been pre-shrunk, machine wash in hot water and detergent. If you can't tell, use cool water and cold-water soap. May use oxygen bleach. Tumble dry with low heat, or air-dry. Press while damp with hot iron, on both sides.	Do not starch. Do not wring or squeeze. Avoid hard water, chlorine bleach, and enzyme products. Susceptible to wrinkling and mildew.
Metallic	Wash by hand in cool water with cold-water soap. Air-dry flat. Press with iron on low heat.	Do not wring or twist. May tear. Avoid heat and bleaches.
Modacrylic	Machine wash with warm water and mild detergent, *or* dry clean. May use oxygen bleach. Tumble dry on low heat. Press with iron on low heat.	May pill or stretch out of shape.
Muslin	A type of weave—*see* Cotton or Synthetic.	
Nylon	Dry clean *or* machine wash with warm water and a mild detergent *or* soap flakes. Rinse well. Wash colored items separately. May use chlorine bleach. Add fabric softener occasionally. Tumble dry on low heat, removing promptly to avoid wrinkles; *or* air dry. Press with warm iron.	Do not wring or twist. Susceptible to static cling. May pill.
Olefin	Dry clean deep-pile fabrics. Machine wash (gentle cycle) with lukewarm water and mild detergent. Add fabric softener occasionally. Tumble dry on low heat, removing promptly to avoid wrinkles. Press with iron on low heat.	Do not wring or twist. Avoid heat and bleaches. May tear.
Organdy	A type of weave—may be cotton or synthetic. Dry clean or wash by hand with cool water and cold-water soap. Roll in a towel to remove excess moisture, and dry flat. Press with cool iron.	Do not wring or twist. Avoid chemicals. May tear.
Permanent press	Machine wash (gentle cycle) with cool to warm water and detergent, *or* dry clean. Add fabric softener occasionally. Tumble dry on low heat, removing promptly to avoid wrinkles; *or* hang to drip dry. Press with warm steam iron.	Avoid extreme temperature changes while fabric is wet. Susceptible to static cling.
Polyester	Machine wash (gentle cycle) with warm water and detergent; *or* dry clean. Add fabric softener occasionally. Tumble dry on low heat, removing promptly to avoid wrinkles. Press on wrong side with steam iron on low heat, *or* while damp.	Avoid extreme temperature changes while fabric is wet. Avoid acetone and amyl acetate. Susceptible to static cling.
Pongee	*See* Silk.	
Rayon	Dry clean or hand wash with lukewarm water and mild detergent *or* soap flakes. Use fabric softener occasionally. May use oxygen bleach. Hang to air-dry. Press on wrong side with warm iron while damp, *or* with a damp pressing cloth.	Do not wring or twist. Do not soak. Avoid chlorine bleach. May shrink or stretch when wet. Susceptible to static cling.
Rubber	Wipe with hot, soapy water. Air-dry. Do not iron.	Avoid heat, bleaches, and greasy creams.

Fabric	To clean and press	Cautions and comments
Saran	Mainly used for garden furniture. Wipe with soapy water. May use bleaches. Air-dry. Do not iron.	Avoid excessive heat.
Satin	A type of weave—may be rayon or synthetic. Dry clean. Press with iron on low heat.	Avoid water. Susceptible to water spots.
Seersucker	A type of weave—see Cotton or Rayon.	
Serge	A type of weave. Dry clean. See Wool.	Rub shiny spots with alcohol.
Sharkskin	An acetate or triacetate. Machine wash with warm water and mild detergent. Tumble dry on high heat, removing promptly to avoid wrinkles. Press with hot steam iron.	Avoid strong alkalis such as washing soda.
Silk	Dry clean. Or, if label indicates it is safe, hand wash in lukewarm water with cold-water soap. Roll in a towel to absorb excess moisture, then air-dry flat. Press on the wrong side with a warm iron while silk is still damp.	Do not wring or twist. Clean promptly—perspiration and dirt weaken silk. Avoid chlorine bleach, enzyme products, heat, and acids such as vinegar or fruit juices. Avoid acetone and amyl acetate. May water spot, shrink, or tear.
Spandex	Hand or machine wash with lukewarm water and cold-water soap. May use oxygen bleach. Tumble dry on low heat. Press with iron on low heat.	Do not wring or twist. Avoid heat, chlorine bleach, sunlight, and greasy creams.
Suede	See Leather.	
Synthetics (general guidelines)	If you aren't certain which synthetic fiber you have, follow these general instructions: Machine wash (gentle cycle) with lukewarm water and a mild detergent or soap flakes. Tumble dry on low heat, removing promptly to avoid wrinkles. Press with iron on low heat.	Before using any special laundry aids or stain removers, test these products on an inconspicuous inside seam. If color runs or fades, do not use.
Taffeta	A type of weave—may be acetate, rayon, or silk. Dry clean or machine wash with warm water and soap flakes. Air-dry flat. Press with iron on low heat.	Do not wring or twist. Avoid heat and bleaches. May tear.
Terrycloth	See Cotton.	
Triacetate	Machine wash (gentle cycle) with warm water and detergent. Tumble dry, removing promptly to avoid wrinkles. Press with hot steam iron.	Do not stretch. Avoid ammonia, acetone, amyl acetate, and other strong chemicals.
Velour	A type of weave—may be cotton or synthetic. Dry clean or machine wash (gentle cycle) with warm water and soap flakes. Wash colored items separately. Tumble dry on low heat. Press on wrong side with iron on low heat.	Do not wring or twist. Avoid acids such as vinegar or fruit juice. Avoid alkalis such as washing soda.
Velvet	A type of weave—may be nylon, silk, or synthetic. Dry clean. Press on wrong side with iron on low heat, or with a damp pressing cloth.	Do not rub. May mat.
Velveteen	A type of weave—may be cotton or synthetic. Dry clean or machine wash with warm water and soap flakes. Tumble dry on low heat. Press on the wrong side with iron on low heat, or with a damp pressing cloth.	Do not rub. May shrink.
Wool	Dry clean or hand wash with cool water and cold-water soap. Rinse with cold water. Roll in a towel to absorb excess moisture, then air-dry flat, away from heat. Press with a warm steam iron or damp pressing cloth.	Do not wring or twist. Avoid soaking, extremes of temperature, chlorine bleach, enzyme products, and ammonia. Avoid acetone and amyl acetate. May shrink or stretch.

STAINS

Wine spill
on carpet

The agents recommended in this chart will act on the stains themselves. However, because the agents could damage certain fabrics, read the descriptions and comments about agents on pages 10–15 before using. If you are still in doubt about the safety for your fabric or material, check the Fabric Care chart on pages 38–41, and test the agent on an inside seam or other inconspicuous spot. The gentlest or mildest agent is always suggested first in this chart. If this is the only agent safe for your fabric, keep repeating this step until the stain is gone. Whenever possible, alternatives are mentioned. If you have set a stain with hot water or with the heat of a clothes dryer, or if the stain is old, you may not be able to get it out at all. In this case, consult a professional. In all cases, bear in mind that removing stains requires patience and repetition.

Stain	Washable Fabrics	Non-Washable Fabrics, Carpets, & Upholstery
Acids (battery, chemistry sets)	**Agents:** Ammonia* ☐Rinse or flush with cool water, then sponge repeatedly with equal parts ammonia and water. Rinse and wash.	**Agents:** Baking soda; ammonia* ☐Sprinkle with baking soda to absorb liquids. Let sit for half an hour, then brush off. Sponge repeatedly with equal parts ammonia and water, then sponge off and blot dry.
Alcoholic Beverages	**Agents:** Club soda; pre-wash product; enzyme product* or washing soda; bleach* ☐Sponge with club soda, then wash. If stain remains, spray with pre-wash product, then wash. If stain still remains, soak for half an hour in water and enzyme product or washing soda, then wash. If necessary, bleach.	**Agents:** Club soda; enzyme product* ☐Sponge repeatedly with club soda, then blot dry. If stain remains, cover with a cloth dampened in water and enzyme product. Keep damp for half an hour, then sponge off and blot dry. If stain still remains, bleach.
Antiperspirant	**Agents:** Pre-wash product; detergent and vinegar or ammonia*; or washing soda ☐Spray with pre-wash product, then wash. If stain remains, soak for half an hour in 1 qt water, 1 tbsp detergent, and 1 tbsp vinegar or ammonia, or water and washing soda. Then wash.	**Agents:** Glycerine, liquid detergent, and vinegar or ammonia* ☐Cover with a cloth dampened in ½ c water, 1 tbsp glycerine, ½ tsp liquid detergent, and 1 tsp vinegar or ammonia. Keep damp for half an hour, then sponge off and blot dry.
Baby Formula, Spit Up	**Agents:** Pre-wash product; enzyme product* or washing soda ☐Spray with pre-wash product, then wash. If stain remains, soak in water and enzyme product or washing soda for half an hour, then wash.	**Agents:** Enzyme product* ☐Cover with a cloth dampened in water and enzyme product. Keep damp for half an hour, then sponge off and blot dry.
Blood	**Agents:** Glycerine; pre-wash product; enzyme product* or washing soda; hydrogen peroxide* and ammonia*; rust remover* ☐Soften old stains with warm glycerine. Rinse in cool water. Spray with pre-wash product, then wash. If stain remains, soak in water and enzyme product or washing soda, then wash. If stain still remains, sponge with hydrogen peroxide with a few drops of ammonia added, and rinse off as soon as stain is bleached; or use a commercial rust remover.	**Agents:** Glycerine; enzyme product* or liquid detergent and ammonia*; hydrogen peroxide* and ammonia*; rust remover* ☐Soften old stains with warm glycerine. Sponge with cool water. Sponge with a solution of water and enzyme product or ½ c water, ½ tsp detergent, and 1 tsp ammonia. Then sponge off and blot dry. If stain remains, dampen with hydrogen peroxide, add a few drops ammonia, and sponge off as soon as stain is bleached; or use a commercial rust remover.
Butter	**Agents:** Pre-wash product; detergent and vinegar or ammonia*; or washing soda ☐Spray with pre-wash product, then wash. If stain remains, soak for half an hour in soapy water with vinegar or ammonia added, or water and washing soda. Then wash.	**Agents:** Pre-wash product; liquid detergent and vinegar or ammonia* ☐Spray with pre-wash product, then sponge off and blot dry. If stain remains, sponge with solution of ½ c water, ½ tsp liquid detergent, and 1 tsp vinegar or ammonia. Repeat until stain is gone, then sponge off and blot dry.
Candy (except chocolate)	**Agents:** Pre-wash product; ammonia* or washing soda; bleach* ☐Spray with pre-wash product, then wash with ½ c ammonia or washing soda added to wash cycle. If stain still remains, bleach.	**Agents:** Pre-wash product; ammonia* or alcohol*; bleach* ☐Spray with pre-wash product, sponge off and blot dry. If stain remains, sponge repeatedly with equal parts ammonia or alcohol and water, then sponge off and blot dry. If stain still remains, bleach.

Chocolate
on shirt

Stain	Washable Fabrics	Non-Washable Fabrics, Carpets, & Upholstery
Catsup	**Agents:** Pre-wash product; washing soda *or* ammonia*; enzyme product* ☐Spray with pre-wash product, then wash with ½ c washing soda *or* ammonia added to wash cycle. If stain remains, soak for half an hour in water and enzyme product, then wash.	**Agents:** Pre-wash product; enzyme product* *or* liquid detergent and ammonia*; alcohol* ☐Spray with pre-wash product, then sponge off and blot dry. If stain remains, sponge repeatedly with a solution of water and enzyme product, *or* ½ c water, ½ tsp detergent, and 1 tsp ammonia, then sponge off and blot dry. If stain still remains, sponge repeatedly with alcohol, then blot dry.
Cheese	**Agents:** Pre-wash product; washing soda ☐Spray with pre-wash product, then wash with ½ c washing soda added to wash cycle.	**Agents:** Pre-wash product; ammonia* *or* alcohol* ☐Spray with pre-wash product, sponge off and blot dry. If stain remains, sponge repeatedly with equal parts ammonia *or* alcohol and water, then sponge off and blot dry.
Chewing Gum	**Agents:** Ice cubes; pre-wash product; dry-cleaning fluid* and mineral oil ☐Freeze with an ice cube held in a plastic bag. Break up frozen gum with a hammer. Spray or sponge with pre-wash product, then wash. If stain remains, cover with a cloth dampened with ¼ c dry-cleaning fluid and 1½ tsp mineral oil. Keep damp for half an hour, then rinse.	**Agents:** Ice cubes; liquid detergent and ammonia*; dry-cleaning fluid* and mineral oil ☐Freeze with an ice cube held in a plastic bag. Break up frozen gum with a hammer. Sponge repeatedly with a solution of ½ c water, ½ tsp detergent, and 1 tsp ammonia. Sponge off and blot dry. If stain remains, cover with a cloth dampened in ¼ c dry-cleaning fluid and 1½ tsp mineral oil. Keep damp for half an hour, then sponge off and blot dry.
Chlorine	Consult a professional cleaner for color removal and dyeing.	Consult a professional cleaner for color removal and dyeing.
Chocolate	**Agents:** Pre-wash product; enzyme product* *or* washing soda; hydrogen peroxide* and ammonia* ☐Spray with pre-wash product, then wash. If stain remains, soak in water and enzyme product *or* washing soda for half an hour, then wash. If stain still remains, flush with hydrogen peroxide, add a few drops ammonia, and rinse as soon as stain is bleached.	**Agents:** Pre-wash product; enzyme product* *or* glycerine, liquid detergent, and ammonia*; alcohol*; hydrogen peroxide* and ammonia* ☐Spray with pre-wash product; sponge off and blot dry. If stain remains, cover with a cloth dampened in enzyme product dissolved in water, *or* a solution of ½ c water, 1 tbsp glycerine, ½ tsp detergent, and 1 tsp ammonia. Keep damp for half an hour, then sponge off and blot dry. If stain still remains, sponge repeatedly with alcohol, then blot dry. If necessary, bleach as for washable fabrics.
Cigarette Burn	**Agents:** Dry-cleaning fluid* and mineral oil; hydrogen peroxide* and ammonia* ☐Cover with a cloth dampened in ¼ c dry-cleaning fluid and 1½ tsp mineral oil. Keep damp for half an hour, then rinse. If stain remains, sponge with hydrogen peroxide, add a few drops ammonia, and watch carefully until stain is gone. Then rinse.	**Agents:** Dry-cleaning fluid* and mineral oil; hydrogen peroxide* and ammonia* ☐Cover with a cloth dampened in ¼ c dry-cleaning fluid and 1½ tsp mineral oil. Keep damp for half an hour, then sponge off and blot dry. If stain remains, sponge with hydrogen peroxide, add a few drops ammonia, and watch carefully until stain is gone. Then sponge off and blot dry.
Coffee	**Agents:** Pre-wash product; enzyme product* or washing soda; bleach* ☐Spray with pre-wash product, then wash. If stain remains, soak for half an hour in water and enzyme product *or* washing soda, then wash. If stain still remains, bleach.	**Agents:** Pre-wash product; enzyme product* or glycerine, liquid detergent, and ammonia*; alcohol* ☐Spray with pre-wash product, then sponge off and blot dry. If stain remains, cover with a cloth dampened in enzyme product dissolved in water, *or* a solution of ½ c water, 1 tbsp glycerine, ½ tsp detergent, and 1 tsp ammonia. Keep damp for half an hour, then sponge off and blot dry. If stain still remains, sponge repeatedly with alcohol.

*These stain-removing agents require special guidelines. All of them are potentially harmful to some fabrics or materials, so before using them, look up the individual agent on pages 10–15. There are a number of products that can be used as bleaching agents. The section on bleaches (page 11) will help you decide which to use. If you're still uncertain about using a particular agent on a fabric or material, check the Fabric Care chart on pages 38–41.

STAINS

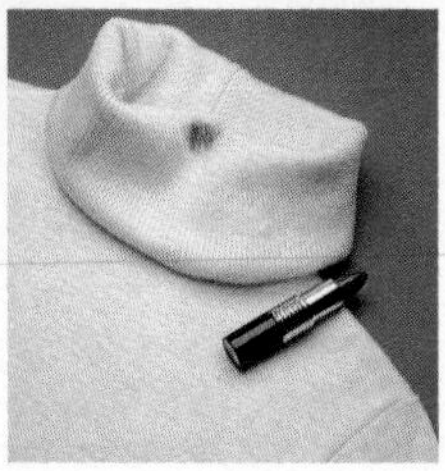

Lipstick
on sweater

Stain	Washable Fabrics	Non-Washable Fabrics, Carpets, & Upholstery
Correction Fluid	**Agents:** Dry-cleaning fluid*; amyl acetate*; bleach* ☐Sponge repeatedly with dry-cleaning fluid, then rinse. If stain remains, sponge repeatedly with amyl acetate, then rinse. If stain still remains, bleach.	**Agents:** Dry-cleaning fluid* and mineral oil; amyl acetate*; bleach* ☐Cover with a cloth dampened in ¼ c dry-cleaning fluid and 1½ tsp mineral oil. Keep damp for half an hour, then sponge off and blot dry. If stain remains, sponge repeatedly with amyl acetate, then sponge off and blot dry. If stain still remains, bleach.
Cosmetics	**Agents:** Pre-wash product; washing soda *or* ammonia*; dry-cleaning fluid*; bleach* ☐Spray with pre-wash product, then wash with ½ c washing soda *or* ammonia added to wash cycle. If stain remains, sponge repeatedly with dry-cleaning fluid, then rinse and wash. If stain still remains, bleach.	**Agents:** Pre-wash product; ammonia* *or* alcohol*; dry-cleaning fluid*; bleach* ☐Spray with pre-wash product, then sponge off and blot dry. If stain remains, sponge repeatedly with a solution of equal parts water and ammonia *or* alcohol, then sponge off and blot dry. If stain still remains, sponge repeatedly with dry-cleaning fluid, then sponge off and blot dry. If necessary, bleach.
Crayon	**Agents:** Ice cubes; pre-wash product; washing soda; bleach* ☐Harden wax crayons with ice cubes held in a plastic bag; remove excess wax. Spray or sponge with pre-wash product, then wash, adding ½ c washing soda to wash cycle. If stain remains, bleach.	**Agents:** Ice cubes; glycerine, liquid detergent, and ammonia*; bleach* ☐Harden wax crayons with ice cubes held in a plastic bag; remove excess wax. Cover with a cloth dampened in ½ c water, 1 tbsp glycerine, ½ tsp detergent, and 1 tsp ammonia. Keep damp for half an hour, then sponge off and blot dry. If stain remains, bleach.
Cream	**Agents:** Pre-wash product; washing soda ☐Spray with pre-wash product, then wash with ½ c washing soda added to wash cycle.	**Agents:** Pre-wash product; vinegar *or* ammonia* ☐Spray with pre-wash product, then sponge off and blot dry. If stain remains, sponge repeatedly with a solution of equal parts water and vinegar *or* ammonia, then sponge off and blot dry.
Creosote	**Agents:** Dry-cleaning fluid* and mineral oil; bleach* ☐Cover with a cloth dampened in ¼ c dry-cleaning fluid and 1½ tsp mineral oil. Keep damp for half an hour, then rinse. If stain remains, bleach.	**Agents:** Dry-cleaning fluid* and mineral oil; bleach* ☐Cover with a cloth dampened in ¼ c dry-cleaning fluid and 1½ tsp mineral oil. Keep damp for half an hour, then sponge off and blot dry. If stain remains, bleach.
Dyes (fabric, shoe, and hair)	**Agents:** Dry-cleaning fluid* and mineral oil; alcohol*; acetone* *or* amyl acetate*; bleach* ☐Cover with a cloth dampened in ¼ c dry-cleaning fluid and 1½ tsp mineral oil. Keep damp for half an hour, then rinse. If stain remains, sponge repeatedly with alcohol, then rinse. If stain still remains, sponge repeatedly with acetone *or* amyl acetate until stain is gone; *or* bleach.	**Agents:** Dry-cleaning fluid* and mineral oil; alcohol*; acetone* *or* amyl acetate*; bleach* ☐Cover with cloth dampened in ¼ c dry-cleaning fluid and 1½ tsp mineral oil. Keep damp for half an hour, then sponge off and blot dry. If stain remains, sponge repeatedly with alcohol, then blot dry. If stain still remains, sponge with acetone *or* amyl acetate until stain is gone, then sponge off and blot dry; *or* bleach.
Eggs	**Agents:** Enzyme product* *or* washing soda; ammonia* ☐Soak for half an hour in enzyme product *or* washing soda, then wash. If stain remains, add ½ c ammonia to the wash cycle.	**Agents:** Enzyme product*; glycerine, liquid detergent, and ammonia*; bleach* ☐Sponge with solution of water and enzyme product, *or* cover with a cloth dampened in ½ c water, 1 tbsp glycerine, ½ tsp detergent, and 1 tsp ammonia. Keep damp for half an hour, then sponge off and blot dry. If stain remains, bleach.
Excrement	**Agents:** Enzyme product* *or* washing soda; ammonia* and vinegar ☐Soak for half an hour in water and enzyme product *or* washing soda. Then wash, adding ½ c ammonia to wash cycle, and 1 c vinegar to final rinse.	**Agents:** Enzyme product*; vinegar *or* ammonia*; alcohol* ☐Sponge with solution of water and enzyme product, *or* with equal parts vinegar *or* ammonia and water. If stain remains, sponge repeatedly with alcohol, then blot dry.

Frosting
on apron

Stain	Washable Fabrics	Non-Washable Fabrics, Carpets, & Upholstery
Fingernail Polish	**Agents:** Dry-cleaning fluid* and mineral oil; acetone*; bleach* ☐Cover with a cloth dampened in ¼ c dry-cleaning fluid and 1½ tsp mineral oil. Keep damp for half an hour, then rinse. If stain remains, sponge repeatedly with acetone. If stain still remains, bleach.	**Agents:** Dry-cleaning fluid* and mineral oil; acetone*; bleach* ☐Cover with a cloth dampened in ¼ c dry-cleaning fluid and 1½ tsp mineral oil. Keep damp for half an hour, then sponge off and blot dry. If stain remains, sponge repeatedly with acetone until stain is gone, then sponge off and blot dry; or bleach.
Fish	**Agents:** Pre-wash product; enzyme product* *or* washing soda ☐Spray with pre-wash product, then wash. If stain remains, soak for half an hour in water and enzyme product *or* washing soda, then wash.	**Agents:** Liquid detergent and ammonia* ☐Sponge repeatedly with a solution of ½ c water, ½ tsp detergent, and 1 tsp ammonia, then sponge off and blot dry.
Food Coloring	**Agents:** Dry-cleaning fluid* and mineral oil; acetone* *or* amyl acetate*; bleach* ☐Cover with a cloth dampened in ¼ c dry-cleaning fluid and 1½ tsp mineral oil. Keep damp for half an hour, then rinse. If stain remains, sponge repeatedly with acetone *or* amyl acetate, then rinse. If stain still remains, bleach.	**Agents:** Dry-cleaning fluid* and mineral oil; acetone* *or* amyl acetate*; bleach* ☐Cover with a cloth dampened in ¼ c dry-cleaning fluid and 1½ tsp mineral oil. Keep damp for half an hour, then sponge off and blot dry. If stain remains, sponge repeatedly with acetone *or* amyl acetate, then sponge off and blot dry. If stain still remains, bleach.
Frosting	**Agents:** Pre-wash product; dry-cleaning fluid* and mineral oil; bleach* ☐Spray or sponge with pre-wash product, then wash. If stain remains, cover with a cloth dampened in ¼ c dry-cleaning fluid and 1½ tsp mineral oil. Keep damp for half an hour, then rinse. If stain still remains, bleach.	**Agents:** Glycerine, liquid detergent, and ammonia*; dry-cleaning fluid*; bleach* ☐Cover with a cloth dampened in ½ c water, 1 tbsp glycerine, ½ tsp detergent, and 1 tsp ammonia. Keep damp for half an hour, then sponge off and blot dry. If stain remains, sponge with dry-cleaning fluid or bleach, then sponge off and blot dry.
Fruit and Fruit Juices	**Agents:** Pre-wash product; enzyme product* *or* washing soda; dry-cleaning fluid*; bleach* ☐Rinse in cool water. Spray with pre-wash product, then wash. If stain remains, soak for half an hour in water and enzyme product *or* washing soda, then wash. If stain still remains, sponge repeatedly with dry-cleaning fluid; blot, then wash. If necessary, bleach.	**Agents:** Pre-wash product; glycerine, liquid detergent, and ammonia*; dry-cleaning fluid*; bleach* ☐Sponge with cool water. Spray with pre-wash product, then sponge off and blot dry. If stain remains, cover with a cloth dampened in ½ c water, 1 tbsp glycerine, ½ tsp detergent, and 1 tsp ammonia. Then sponge off and blot dry. If stain still remains, sponge repeatedly with dry-cleaning fluid, then sponge off and blot dry. If necessary, bleach.
Furniture and Floor Polish or Wax	**Agents:** Dry-cleaning fluid* and mineral oil; pre-wash product; bleach* ☐Cover with a cloth dampened in ¼ c dry-cleaning fluid and 1½ tsp mineral oil. Keep damp for half an hour, then rinse. If stain remains, spray or sponge with pre-wash product, and wash. If stain still remains, bleach.	**Agents:** Dry-cleaning fluid* and mineral oil; liquid detergent and ammonia*; bleach* ☐Cover with a cloth dampened in ¼ c dry-cleaning fluid and 1½ tsp mineral oil. Keep damp for half an hour, then sponge off and blot dry. If stain remains, sponge repeatedly with soapy water with ammonia added; or bleach. Sponge off and blot dry.
Gelatine	**Agents:** Enzyme product* *or* washing soda; ammonia*; dry-cleaning fluid* ☐Soak for half an hour in water and enzyme product *or* washing soda, then wash, adding ½ c ammonia to the wash cycle. If stain remains, sponge repeatedly with dry-cleaning fluid, blot, and wash.	**Agents:** Liquid detergent and ammonia*; enzyme product*; dry-cleaning fluid* ☐Sponge first with cool water, then with a solution of ½ c water, ½ tsp detergent, and 1 tsp ammonia. Sponge off and blot dry. If stain remains, sponge with water and enzyme product, then sponge off and blot dry. If stain still remains, sponge repeatedly with dry-cleaning fluid, sponge off, and blot dry.

*These stain-removing agents require special guidelines. All of them are potentially harmful to some fabrics or materials, so before using them, look up the individual agent on pages 10–15. There are a number of products that can be used as bleaching agents. The section on bleaches (page 11) will help you decide which to use. If you're still uncertain about using a particular agent on a fabric or material, check the Fabric Care chart on pages 38–41.

STAINS

Grass stains
on jeans

Stain	Washable Fabrics	Non-Washable Fabrics, Carpets, & Upholstery
Graphite	**Agents:** Dry-cleaning fluid*; bleach* ☐Brush off excess graphite. Sponge repeatedly with dry-cleaning fluid, then rinse. If stain remains, bleach.	**Agents:** Dry-cleaning fluid*; bleach* ☐Brush off excess graphite. Sponge repeatedly with dry-cleaning fluid, then sponge off and blot dry. If stain remains, bleach.
Grass	**Agents:** Pre-wash product; washing soda; dry-cleaning fluid* and mineral oil; amyl acetate* ☐Spray with pre-wash product, then wash with ½ c washing soda added to wash cycle. If stain remains, cover with a cloth dampened in ¼ c dry-cleaning fluid and 1½ tsp mineral oil. Keep damp for half an hour, then rinse and wash. If stain still remains, sponge with amyl acetate, and rinse off as soon as stain is gone.	**Agents:** Pre-wash product; dry-cleaning fluid* and mineral oil; amyl acetate* ☐Spray with pre-wash product, then sponge off and blot dry. If stain remains, cover with a cloth dampened in ¼ c dry-cleaning fluid and 1½ tsp mineral oil. Keep damp for half an hour, then sponge off and blot dry. If stain still remains, sponge with amyl acetate. Sponge off as soon as stain is gone, and blot dry.
Gravy	**Agents:** Pre-wash product; washing soda *or* ammonia* ☐Spray with pre-wash product, then wash with ½ c washing soda *or* ammonia added to wash cycle.	**Agents:** Pre-wash product; liquid detergent and ammonia*; alcohol* ☐Spray with pre-wash product, then sponge off and blot dry. If stain remains, sponge repeatedly with a solution of ½ c water, ½ tsp detergent, and 1 tsp ammonia, then sponge off and blot dry. If stain still remains, sponge repeatedly with alcohol, blot dry.
Grease	**Agents:** Bar soap; pre-wash product; washing soda *or* ammonia* ☐Rub stain with bar soap, rinse, and repeat until stain is gone. If stain remains, spray with pre-wash product, then wash with ½ c washing soda *or* ammonia added to wash cycle.	**Agents:** Pre-wash product; liquid detergent and ammonia*; alcohol* ☐Spray with pre-wash product, then sponge off and blot dry. If stain remains, sponge repeatedly with a solution of ½ c water, ½ tsp detergent, and 1 tsp ammonia, then sponge off and blot dry. If stain still remains, sponge repeatedly with alcohol, then blot dry.
Ice cream	**Agents:** Pre-wash product; enzyme product* *or* washing soda ☐Spray with pre-wash product; then wash. If stain remains, soak for half an hour in water and enzyme product *or* washing soda, then wash.	**Agents:** Pre-wash product; enzyme product* *or* liquid detergent and ammonia*; alcohol* ☐Spray with pre-wash product, then sponge off and blot dry. If stain remains, sponge with a solution of water and enzyme product, *or* ½ c water, ½ tsp detergent, and 1 tsp ammonia, then sponge off and blot dry. If stain still remains, sponge repeatedly with alcohol, then blot dry.
Inks (ballpoint pen, indelible pencil, felt-tip marker, typewriter ribbon, India ink, newspaper, duplicating)	**Agents:** Glycerine *or* hair spray; dry-cleaning fluid* and mineral oil; acetone* *or* amyl acetate* ☐Soften with warm glycerine or hair spray, then wash. If stain remains, cover with a cloth dampened with ¼ c dry-cleaning fluid and 1½ tsp mineral oil. Keep damp for half an hour, then rinse. If stain remains, sponge with acetone *or* amyl acetate until stain is gone.	**Agents:** Glycerine *or* hair spray; dry-cleaning fluid* and mineral oil; acetone* *or* amyl acetate* ☐Soften with warm glycerine *or* hair spray, then sponge off and blot dry. If stain remains, cover with a cloth dampened with ¼ c dry-cleaning fluid and 1½ tsp mineral oil. Keep damp for half an hour, then rinse. If stain remains, sponge with acetone *or* amyl acetate until stain is gone.
Margarine	**Agents:** Pre-wash product; washing soda *or* ammonia* ☐Spray with pre-wash product, then wash with ½ c washing soda or ammonia added to wash cycle.	**Agents:** Pre-wash product; liquid detergent and ammonia* ☐Spray with pre-wash product; sponge off and blot dry. If stain remains, sponge with a solution of ½ c water, ½ tsp detergent, and 1 tsp ammonia, then sponge off and blot dry.
Mayonnaise	**Agents:** Pre-wash product; washing soda *or* ammonia*; vinegar ☐Spray with pre-wash product, then wash with ½ c washing soda *or* ammonia added to wash cycle, and 1 c vinegar added to final rinse.	**Agents:** Pre-wash product, liquid detergent, and vinegar *or* ammonia* ☐Spray with pre-wash product, then sponge off and blot dry. If stain remains, sponge repeatedly with a solution of ½ c water, ½ tsp detergent, and 1 tsp vinegar *or* ammonia, then sponge off and blot dry.

Paint on
sweatshirt

Stain	Washable Fabrics	Non-Washable Fabrics, Carpets, & Upholstery
Medicines (cough syrup, mercurochrome/ merthiolate, nose drops, oint- ments/salves, penicillin, vitamins)	**Agents:** Glycerine; pre-wash product; washing soda *or* ammonia*; alcohol*; bleach* ☐Soften stain with warm glycerine. Spray with pre- wash product, then wash with ½ c washing soda *or* ammonia added to wash cycle. If stain remains, sponge repeatedly with alcohol, then wash. If stain still remains, bleach.	**Agents:** Glycerine; pre-wash product; liquid detergent and ammonia*; alcohol*; bleach* ☐Soften stain with warm glycerine. Spray with prewash product, then sponge off and blot dry. If stain remains, sponge repeatedly with a solution of ½ c water, ½ tsp detergent, and 1 tsp ammonia, then sponge off and blot dry. If stain still remains, bleach.
Mildew	**Agents:** Chlorine bleach* *or* disinfectant liquid; alcohol*; bleach* ☐If chlorine is safe for fabric, soak for 15 minutes in a mild solution of chlorine bleach and water, then wash; *or* wash in hottest water safe for fabric, adding ½ c disinfectant liquid to wash cycle. If stain remains, sponge repeatedly with alcohol, then wash. If stain still remains, bleach again.	**Agents:** Chlorine bleach *or* disinfectant liquid; alcohol*; bleach* ☐If chlorine is safe for fabric, sponge repeatedly with a mild solution of chlorine bleach and water, *or* with a mild solution of disinfectant liquid and water. Then sponge off and blot dry. If stain remains, sponge repeatedly with alcohol, then blot dry.
Mud	**Agents:** Enzyme product*; bleach* *or* rust remover* ☐Let dry, then gently brush off excess mud. Soak for half an hour in water and enzyme product, then wash. If stain remains, use bleach or a commercial rust remover made for fabrics.	**Agents:** Enzyme product*; bleach* *or* rust remover* ☐Let dry, then gently brush off excess mud. Cover with a cloth dampened in water and enzyme product. Let sit for half an hour, then sponge off and blot dry. If stain remains, use bleach *or* a commercial rust remover made for fabrics.
Mustard	**Agents:** Glycerine; washing soda and vinegar; dry-cleaning fluid* and mineral oil; alcohol*; bleach* ☐Soften stain with warm glycerine. Wash as usual with ½ c washing soda added to wash cycle, and 1 c vinegar added to final rinse. If stain remains, cover with a cloth dampened in ¼ c dry-cleaning fluid and 1½ tsp mineral oil. Keep damp for half an hour, then wash. If stain still remains, sponge repeatedly with alcohol, then wash. If necessary, bleach.	**Agents:** Glycerine; dry-cleaning fluid* and mineral oil; alcohol*; bleach* ☐Soften stain with warm glycerine. Cover with a cloth dampened with ¼ c dry-cleaning fluid and 1½ tsp mineral oil. Keep damp for half an hour, then sponge off and blot dry. If stain remains, sponge repeatedly with alcohol, then blot dry. If stain still remains, bleach.
Oils (bath, castor, coconut, cod-liver, cooking—corn, peanut, olive, safflower, soy— linseed, lubricating)	**Agents:** Pre-wash product; washing soda *or* ammonia*; vinegar; dry-cleaning fluid* ☐Spray with pre-wash product, and wash with ½ c washing soda *or* ammonia added to wash cycle, and 1 c vinegar added to final rinse. If stain remains, sponge repeatedly with dry-cleaning fluid, then rinse and wash.	**Agents:** Pre-wash product; liquid detergent and vinegar *or* ammonia*; dry-cleaning fluid* ☐Spray with pre-wash product, then sponge off and blot dry. If stain remains, sponge repeatedly with a solution of ½ c water, ½ tsp detergent, and 1 tsp vinegar *or* ammonia, then sponge off and blot dry. If stain still remains, sponge repeatedly with dry- cleaning fluid, then sponge off and blot dry.
Paint (oil-based)	**Agents:** Ammonia*; paint thinner *or* dry-cleaning fluid* ☐Sponge repeatedly with ammonia, then wash. If stain remains, sponge repeatedly with the paint thinner recommended on paint label, *or* with dry-cleaning fluid. Then wash.	**Agents:** Ammonia*; paint thinner *or* dry-cleaning fluid* ☐Sponge repeatedly with ammonia, then sponge off and blot dry. If stain remains, sponge repeatedly with the paint thinner recommended on paint label, *or* with dry-cleaning fluid. Then sponge off and blot dry.
Paint (water-based)	**Agents:** Glycerine; washing soda *or* ammonia*; amyl acetate* ☐Soften stain with warm glycerine. Wash as usual, with ½ c washing soda *or* ammonia added to wash cycle. If stain remains, sponge with amyl acetate, then wash.	**Agents:** Glycerine; ammonia*; amyl acetate* ☐Soften stain with warm glycerine. Sponge repeatedly with equal parts ammonia and water, then sponge off and blot dry. If stain remains, sponge with amyl acetate, then sponge off and blot dry.

*These stain-removing agents require special guidelines. All of them are potentially harmful to some fabrics or materials, so before using them, look up the individual agent on pages 10–15. There are a number of products that can be used as bleaching agents. The section on bleaches (page 11) will help you decide which to use. If you're still uncertain about using a particular agent on a fabric or material, check the Fabric Care chart on pages 38–41.

STAINS

Salad dressing
on tablecloth

Stain	Washable Fabrics	Non-Washable Fabrics, Carpets, & Upholstery
Pencil Lead	**Agents:** Art gum eraser; hair spray; washing soda *or* ammonia* ☐Rub off with art gum eraser. If stain remains, spray with hair spray, then wash, adding ½ c washing soda *or* ½ c ammonia to wash cycle.	**Agents:** Art gum eraser; hair spray; liquid detergent and ammonia*; bleach* ☐Rub off with art gum eraser. If stain remains, spray with hair spray, then sponge off and blot dry. If stain still remains, sponge repeatedly with solution of ½ c water, ½ tsp detergent, and 1 tsp ammonia, then sponge off and blot dry. If necessary, bleach.
Permanent-wave Solution	**Agents:** Pre-wash product; alcohol*; enzyme product* *or* washing soda ☐Spray with pre-wash product, then wash. If stain remains, sponge repeatedly with alcohol, and blot. If stain still remains, soak for half an hour in water and enzyme product *or* washing soda, then wash.	**Agents:** Pre-wash product; alcohol*; enzyme product* *or* liquid detergent and vinegar ☐Spray with pre-wash product, then sponge off and blot dry. If stain remains, sponge repeatedly with alcohol, then blot dry. If stain still remains, cover with a cloth dampened in water and enzyme product, *or* in a solution of ½ c water, ½ tsp detergent, and 1 tsp vinegar. Keep damp for half an hour, then sponge off and blot dry.
Perspiration	**Agents:** Pre-wash product; washing soda *or* ammonia* and vinegar; alcohol* ☐Spray with pre-wash product, and wash with ½ c washing soda *or* ammonia added to wash cycle, and 1 c vinegar added to final rinse. If stain remains, sponge repeatedly with alcohol, then wash.	**Agents:** Pre-wash product; liquid detergent and vinegar *or* ammonia*; alcohol* ☐Spray with pre-wash product, then sponge off and blot dry. If stain remains, cover with a cloth dampened in a solution of ½ c water, ½ tsp liquid detergent, and 1 tsp vinegar *or* ammonia. Keep damp for half an hour, then sponge off and blot dry. If stain still remains, sponge repeatedly with alcohol, then blot dry.
Rust	**Agents:** Dry-cleaning fluid* and mineral oil; hydrogen peroxide* and ammonia*; rust remover for fabrics* ☐Cover with a cloth dampened in ¼ c dry-cleaning fluid and 1½ tsp mineral oil. Keep damp for half an hour, then sponge with hydrogen peroxide, add a few drops ammonia, and rinse as soon as stain is bleached; *or* use a commercial rust remover made for fabrics, available at some fabric stores.	**Agents:** Dry-cleaning fluid* and mineral oil; hydrogen peroxide* and ammonia*; rust remover for fabrics* ☐Cover with a cloth dampened in ¼ c dry-cleaning fluid and 1½ tsp mineral oil. Keep damp for half an hour, then sponge off and blot dry. If stain remains, sponge with hydrogen peroxide, add a few drops ammonia, and sponge off as soon as stain is bleached; *or* use a commercial rust remover made for fabrics, available at some fabric stores.
Salad Dressing	**Agents:** Pre-wash product; enzyme product* *or* washing soda; ammonia* ☐Spray with pre-wash product, then wash. If stain remains, soak for half an hour in water and enzyme product *or* washing soda, then wash. If stain still remains, sponge repeatedly with equal parts ammonia and water, then wash.	**Agents:** Pre-wash product; enzyme product* *or* liquid detergent and ammonia*; bleach* ☐Spray with pre-wash product, then sponge off and blot dry. If stain remains, cover with a cloth dampened in water and enzyme product, or a solution of ½ c water, ½ tsp detergent, and 1 tsp ammonia. Keep damp for half an hour, then sponge off and blot dry. If necessary, bleach.
Salt Water	**Agents:** Pre-wash product; vinegar ☐Spray with pre-wash product, then wash, adding 1 c vinegar to final rinse.	**Agents:** Pre-wash product; liquid detergent and vinegar ☐Spray with pre-wash product, then sponge off and blot dry. If stain remains, sponge repeatedly with a solution of ½ c water, ½ tsp detergent, and 1 tsp vinegar, then sponge off and blot dry.
Sauces	**Agents:** Pre-wash product; enzyme product* *or* washing soda; vinegar; bleach* ☐Spray with pre-wash product, then wash. If stain remains, soak for half an hour in water and enzyme product *or* washing soda, then wash, adding 1 c vinegar to final rinse. If stain still remains, bleach.	**Agents:** Pre-wash product; enzyme product* *or* liquid detergent and vinegar; bleach* ☐Spray with pre-wash product, then sponge off and blot dry. If stain remains, cover with a cloth dampened in water and enzyme product, *or* a solution of ½ c water, ½ tsp detergent, and 1 tsp vinegar. Keep damp for half an hour, then sponge off and blot dry. If stain still remains, bleach.

Scorch mark
on shirt

Stain	Washable Fabrics	Non-Washable Fabrics, Carpets, & Upholstery
Scorch	**Agents:** Hydrogen peroxide* and ammonia* ☐Sponge with hydrogen peroxide, add a few drops ammonia, and rinse as soon as stain is gone. Then wash.	**Agents:** Hydrogen peroxide* and ammonia* ☐Sponge with hydrogen peroxide, add a few drops ammonia, and sponge off as soon as stain is gone. Then blot dry.
Sherbet	**Agents:** Pre-wash product; enzyme product* *or* washing soda; ammonia* ☐Spray with pre-wash product, then wash. If stain remains, soak for half an hour in water and enzyme product *or* washing soda, then wash. If stain still remains, wash with ½ c ammonia added to wash cycle.	**Agents:** Pre-wash product; enzyme product* *or* liquid detergent and ammonia* ☐Spray with pre-wash product, then sponge off and blot dry. If stain remains, cover with a cloth dampened in water and enzyme product, *or* a solution of ½ c water, ½ tsp detergent, and 1 tsp ammonia. Keep damp for half an hour, then sponge off and blot dry.
Shoe Polish (white)	**Agents:** Dry-cleaning fluid* and mineral oil; amyl acetate* ☐Cover with a cloth dampened in ¼ c dry-cleaning fluid and 1½ tsp mineral oil. Keep damp for half an hour, then wash. If stain remains, sponge with amyl acetate until stain is gone, then wash.	**Agents:** Dry-cleaning fluid* and mineral oil; amyl acetate* ☐Cover with a cloth dampened in ¼ c dry-cleaning fluid and 1½ tsp mineral oil. Keep damp for half an hour, then sponge off and blot dry. If stain remains, sponge with amyl acetate until stain is gone.
Shoe Polish (other colors)	**Agents:** Washing soda *or* ammonia*; dry-cleaning fluid*; bleach* ☐Wash as usual, with ½ cup washing soda *or* ammonia added to wash cycle. If stain remains, sponge repeatedly with dry-cleaning fluid, then rinse and wash. If stain still remains, bleach.	**Agents:** Liquid detergent and ammonia*; dry-cleaning fluid*; bleach* ☐Cover with a cloth dampened in ½ c water, 1 tsp detergent, and 1 tsp ammonia. Keep damp for half an hour, then sponge off and blot dry. If stain remains, sponge repeatedly with dry-cleaning fluid.
Smoke/Soot	**Agents:** Pre-wash product; washing soda *or* ammonia*; alcohol*; bleach* ☐Spray with pre-wash product, then wash, adding ½ c washing soda *or* ammonia to wash cycle. If stain remains, sponge repeatedly with alcohol, then wash. If stain still remains, bleach.	**Agents:** Pre-wash product; liquid detergent and ammonia*; alcohol*; bleach* ☐Spray with pre-wash product, then sponge off and blot dry. If stain remains, sponge with a solution of ½ c water, ½ tsp detergent, and 1 tsp ammonia, then sponge off and blot dry. If stain still remains, sponge repeatedly with alcohol, then blot dry.
Soft Drinks	**Agents:** Pre-wash product; enzyme product* *or* washing soda; vinegar ☐Spray with pre-wash product, then wash. If stain remains, soak for half an hour in water and enzyme product *or* washing soda. Then wash, adding 1 c vinegar to final rinse.	**Agents:** Pre-wash product; enzyme product* or liquid detergent and vinegar ☐Spray with pre-wash product, then sponge off and blot dry. If stain remains, cover with a cloth dampened in water and enzyme product, *or* a solution of ½ c water, ½ tsp detergent, and 1 tsp vinegar. Keep damp for half an hour, then sponge off and blot dry.
Solder, Liquid	**Agents:** Dry-cleaning fluid*; amyl acetate*; bleach* ☐Sponge repeatedly with dry-cleaning fluid, then rinse. If stain remains, sponge repeatedly with amyl acetate, then rinse. If stain still remains, bleach.	**Agents:** Dry-cleaning fluid* and mineral oil; amyl acetate*; bleach* ☐Cover with a cloth dampened in ¼ c dry-cleaning fluid and 1½ tsp mineral oil. Keep damp for half an hour, then sponge off and blot dry. If stain remains, sponge repeatedly with amyl acetate, then sponge off and blot dry. If necessary, bleach.
Soups (cream and vegetable)	**Agents:** Enzyme product* *or* washing soda; ammonia* ☐Soak for half an hour in water and enzyme product *or* washing soda, then wash, adding ½ c ammonia to wash cycle.	**Agents:** Enzyme product* *or* liquid detergent and ammonia* ☐Cover with a cloth dampened in water and enzyme product, *or* with a solution of ½ c water, ½ tsp liquid detergent, and 1 tsp ammonia. Keep damp for half an hour, then sponge off and blot dry.

*These stain-removing agents require special guidelines. All of them are potentially harmful to some fabrics or materials, so before using them, look up the individual agent on pages 10–15. There are a number of products that can be used as bleaching agents. The section on bleaches (page 11) will help you decide which to use. If you're still uncertain about using a particular agent on a fabric or material, check the Fabric Care chart on pages 38–41.

STAINS

Tea stain
on napkin

Stain	Washable Fabrics	Non-Washable Fabrics, Carpets, & Upholstery
Soups (meat)	**Agents:** Pre-wash product; enzyme product* or washing soda; ammonia*; vinegar; bleach* ☐Spray with pre-wash product, then wash. If stain remains, soak for half an hour in water and enzyme product or washing soda, then wash. If stain still remains, wash again, adding ½ c ammonia to wash cycle, and 1 c vinegar to final rinse. If necessary, bleach.	**Agents:** Pre-wash product; enzyme product* or liquid detergent and ammonia* or vinegar; bleach* ☐Spray with pre-wash product, then sponge off and blot dry. If stain remains, cover with a cloth dampened in water and enzyme product, or a solution of ½ c water, ½ tsp detergent, and 1 tsp ammonia or vinegar. Keep damp for half an hour, then sponge off and blot dry. If stain remains, bleach.
Syrup	**Agents:** Pre-wash product; ammonia* or washing soda ☐Spray with pre-wash product, then wash with ½ c ammonia or washing soda added to wash cycle.	**Agents:** Pre-wash product; liquid detergent and ammonia*; bleach* ☐Spray with pre-wash product, then sponge off and blot dry. If stain remains, sponge repeatedly with a solution of ½ c water, ½ tsp detergent, and 1 tsp ammonia. Sponge off and blot dry. If stain still remains, bleach.
Tape	**Agents:** Alcohol*; dry-cleaning fluid* and mineral oil; acetone* or amyl acetate* ☐Sponge repeatedly with alcohol, then wash. If stain remains, cover with a cloth dampened in ¼ c dry-cleaning fluid and 1½ tsp mineral oil. Keep damp for half an hour, then rinse. If stain still remains, sponge with acetone or amyl acetate until stain is gone, then wash.	**Agents:** Alcohol*; dry-cleaning fluid* and mineral oil; acetone* or amyl acetate* ☐Sponge repeatedly with alcohol, then blot dry. If stain remains, cover with a cloth dampened in ¼ c dry-cleaning fluid and 1½ tsp mineral oil. Keep damp for half an hour, then sponge off and blot dry. If stain still remains, sponge with acetone or amyl acetate until stain is gone, then sponge off and blot dry.
Tar	**Agents:** Glycerine; dry-cleaning fluid* and mineral oil; bleach* ☐Soften stain with warm glycerine. Cover with a cloth dampened in ¼ c dry-cleaning fluid and 1½ tsp mineral oil. Keep damp for half an hour, then rinse and wash. If stain remains, repeat process, then wash, using bleach if necessary.	**Agents:** Glycerine; dry-cleaning fluid* and mineral oil; bleach* ☐Soften stain with warm glycerine. Cover with a cloth dampened in ¼ c dry-cleaning fluid and 1½ tsp mineral oil. Keep damp for half an hour, then sponge off and blot dry. If stain remains, repeat process. If stain still remains, bleach.
Tea	**Agents:** Pre-wash product; enzyme product* or washing soda; alcohol*; bleach* ☐Spray with pre-wash product, then wash. If stain remains, soak for half an hour in water and enzyme product or washing soda, then wash. If stain still remains, sponge repeatedly with alcohol, then wash. If necessary, bleach.	**Agents:** Pre-wash product; enzyme product* or glycerine, liquid detergent, and ammonia*; alcohol*; bleach* ☐Spray with pre-wash product, then sponge off and blot dry. If stain remains, cover with a cloth dampened in enzyme product dissolved in water, or ½ c water, 1 tbsp glycerine, ½ tsp detergent, and 1 tsp ammonia. Keep damp for half an hour, then sponge off and blot dry. If stain still remains, sponge repeatedly with alcohol, then blot dry. If necessary, bleach.
Tobacco	**Agents:** Pre-wash product; enzyme product* or washing soda; bleach* ☐Spray with pre-wash product, then wash. If stain remains, soak for half an hour in water and enzyme product or washing soda, then wash. If stain still remains, bleach.	**Agents:** Pre-wash product; enzyme product* or liquid detergent and ammonia*; dry-cleaning fluid* ☐Spray with pre-wash product, then sponge off and blot dry. If stain remains, sponge with a solution of water and enzyme product or ½ c water, ½ tsp detergent, and 1 tsp ammonia. Keep damp for half an hour, then sponge off and blot dry. If stain still remains, sponge repeatedly with dry-cleaning fluid, then sponge off and blot dry.
Tomatoes, Tomato Juice	**Agents:** Pre-wash product; enzyme product* or washing soda; ammonia* or vinegar; bleach* ☐Spray with pre-wash product, then wash. If stain remains, soak for half an hour in water and enzyme product or washing soda, then rinse. If stain remains, sponge repeatedly with equal parts water and ammonia or vinegar, then wash. If necessary, bleach.	**Agents:** Pre-wash product; enzyme product* or liquid detergent and ammonia* or vinegar; bleach* ☐Spray with pre-wash product, then sponge off and blot dry. If stain remains, sponge repeatedly with a solution of water and enzyme product, or ½ c water, ½ tsp detergent, and 1 tsp ammonia or vinegar, then sponge off and blot dry. If stain remains, bleach.

Candle wax on tablecloth

Stain	Washable Fabrics	Non-Washable Fabrics, Carpets, & Upholstery
Urine	**Agents:** Pre-wash product; enzyme product* or washing soda; ammonia* ☐Spray with pre-wash product, then wash. If stain remains, soak for half an hour in water and enzyme product or washing soda, then wash. If stain still remains, wash again, adding ½ c ammonia to wash cycle.	**Agents:** Pre-wash product; enzyme product* or liquid detergent and ammonia*; baking soda ☐Spray with pre-wash product, then wash. If stain remains, sponge repeatedly with a solution of water and enzyme product, or ½ c water, ½ tsp detergent, and 1 tsp ammonia, then sponge off and blot dry. On carpets, sprinkle baking soda on stain, leave for several hours, then vacuum before using pre-wash product. A commercial product to remove odor of urine is available at pet shops.
Varnish	**Agents:** Dry-cleaning fluid* and mineral oil; acetone* or amyl acetate*; bleach* ☐Cover with a cloth dampened in ¼ c dry-cleaning fluid and 1½ tsp mineral oil. Keep damp for half an hour, then rinse and wash. If stain remains, sponge repeatedly with acetone or amyl acetate until stain is gone, then wash. If stain still remains, bleach.	**Agents:** Dry-cleaning fluid* and mineral oil; acetone* or amyl acetate*; bleach* ☐Cover with a cloth dampened in ¼ c dry-cleaning fluid and 1½ tsp mineral oil. Keep damp for half an hour, then sponge off and blot dry. If stain remains, sponge repeatedly with acetone or amyl acetate until stain is gone, then sponge off and blot dry. If stain still remains, bleach.
Vegetables, Vegetable Juices	**Agents:** Pre-wash product; enzyme product* or washing soda; ammonia*; bleach* ☐Spray with pre-wash product, then wash. If stain remains, soak for half an hour in water and enzyme product or washing soda, then wash with ½ c ammonia added to wash cycle. If stain still remains, bleach.	**Agents:** Pre-wash product; enzyme product* or liquid detergent and ammonia*; bleach* ☐Spray with pre-wash product, then sponge off. If stain remains, sponge repeatedly with a solution of water and enzyme product, or ½ c water, ½ tsp detergent, and 1 tsp ammonia, then sponge off and blot dry. If stain still remains, bleach.
Vomit	**Agents:** Pre-wash product; enzyme product* or washing soda; ammonia* ☐Spray with pre-wash product, then wash. If stain remains, soak for half an hour in water and enzyme product or washing soda, then wash with ½ c ammonia added to wash cycle.	**Agents:** Pre-wash product; enzyme product* or liquid detergent and ammonia*; alcohol* ☐Spray with pre-wash product, then sponge off and blot dry. If stain remains, sponge with a solution of water and enzyme product, or ½ c water, ½ tsp detergent, and 1 tsp ammonia, then sponge off and blot dry. If stain still remains, sponge repeatedly with alcohol, then blot dry.
Walnut	**Agents:** Glycerine, detergent, and vinegar; bleach* ☐Soften stain with warm glycerine. Wash in detergent with 1 c vinegar added to final rinse. If stain remains, bleach.	**Agents:** Glycerine, liquid detergent, and vinegar; bleach* ☐Soften stain with warm glycerine. Sponge repeatedly with solution of ½ c water, ½ tsp detergent, and 1 tsp vinegar, then sponge off and blot dry. If stain remains, bleach.
Water Spots	**Agents:** Pre-wash product; washing soda; alcohol* ☐Spray with pre-wash product, then wash. If stain remains, soak for half an hour in water and washing soda, then rinse. If stain still remains, sponge repeatedly with alcohol, then wash.	**Agents:** Pre-wash product; alcohol* ☐Spray with pre-wash product, then sponge off and blot dry. If stain remains, sponge repeatedly with alcohol, then blot dry.
Wax	**Agents:** Dry-cleaning fluid* and mineral oil; bleach* ☐Scrape off excess wax. Place stained area between white paper towels, and iron at low temperature. Change paper, and iron again until wax is absorbed. If no stain remains, wash in hottest water possible. If stain remains, cover with a cloth dampened in ¼ c dry-cleaning fluid and 1½ tsp mineral oil. Keep damp for half an hour, then wash. If stain still remains, bleach.	**Agents:** Dry-cleaning fluid* and mineral oil; bleach* ☐Scrape off excess wax. Place white paper towels over stain, then iron at low temperature. Change paper, and iron again until wax is absorbed. If stain remains, sponge with hottest water possible. If stain still remains, cover with a cloth dampened in ¼ c dry-cleaning fluid and 1½ tsp mineral oil. Keep damp for half an hour, then blot dry.

*These stain-removing agents require special guidelines. All of them are potentially harmful to some fabrics or materials, so before using them, look up the individual agent on pages 10–15. There are a number of products that can be used as bleaching agents. The section on bleaches (page 11) will help you decide which to use. If you're still uncertain about using a particular agent on a fabric or material, check the Fabric Care chart on pages 38–41.

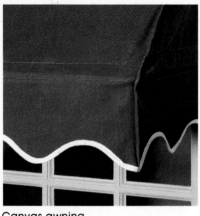

Canvas awning

You can clean most things in your home with a few basic cleaning agents. However, delicate or especially valuable items should be cleaned by a professional.

Acrylics

To clean: Wash with warm, soapy water. If acrylic is especially grimy, add a little ammonia.

To polish and remove scratches: Use a commercial acrylic polish (available from grocery or hardware stores). Avoid acetone (nail polish remover), abrasive pads or powders, and excess heat.

Alabaster

To clean and remove stains: Rub with alcohol, kerosene, bleach, or acetone. Never use water. Restore surface with marble wax.

To protect: Wipe with furniture or marble wax or polish.

Andirons

To remove burned-on resins: Using emery paper (available at hardware stores), rub in one direction. Scrub with hot, soapy water, then polish with brass or copper polish. (This is a tough job, requiring patience.)

To remove rust from iron: Paint with a rust remover/retardant, following manufacturer's directions.

Appliances

See pages 62–65.

Aquariums

To renew the water: Every 3 or 4 weeks, agitate the gravel to suspend dirt and algae, then remove ⅓ of the tank water. Refill with room-temperature tap water, with a water conditioner added (available at pet stores). Follow manufacturer's directions. *Or* use plain tap water, but let it stand for 24 hours to release the chlorine.

To keep down algae growth: Add algae-eating fish to the tank, *or* hand scrub with algae scrubber (available from pet-supply stores), following manufacturer's directions. Don't clean the gravel unless you suspect a parasite or disease problem—uncleaned gravel provides the bacteria necessary for healthy fish.

Artificial flowers

(**Fabric**) *To clean:* Place flowers in a paper bag with 1 c salt. Hold the stems and shake for a couple of minutes. To protect new artificial flowers, spray with hair spray.

(**Plastic**) *To clean:* Swish in liquid detergent and cool water. Rinse, then hang upside down to dry.

Art objects

To clean and repair valuable pieces, consult a professional art restorer. (Ask your local museum or art gallery for a recommendation.)

To clean: See individual material—porcelain, glass, plaster of paris, and so on.

Art prints

Take valuable prints to a professional art restorer for cleaning and repairs. Ask your local museum or art gallery for a recommendation. If the print is unprotected by glass, gently dust its surface with a lamb's wool duster.

Ashtrays

To clean and deodorize: Wipe out ashtrays with a solution of equal parts alcohol and water. Use ammonia to wipe silver ashtrays. (Never use water on alabaster ashtrays.)

Awnings

To clean: Roll out to the most open position. Scrub with a soft brush and a solution of equal parts all-purpose cleaner and water, adding a little chlorine bleach to retard mildew growth. Rinse well, and allow to dry thoroughly before rolling awning up. Protect metal parts from rust with a coat of mineral oil.

Baby bottles

See Bottles.

Balls

(**Golf**) *To clean:* Soak overnight in 1 qt warm water and 1 tbsp ammonia. Rinse, then dry.

(**Leather, Plastic, and Rubber**) *To clean and keep from cracking:* Use a mild detergent and warm water. Wipe with furniture polish *or* saddle soap.

(**Ping Pong**) *To restore dented or deflated balls:* Drop in very hot water for 15 minutes.

(**Tennis**) *To clean:* Dry wet balls in the sun. Gently brush off dirt.

To restore deflated balls: Wrap in aluminum foil and place in a 200°F oven for 15 minutes.

Barbecue grills

To clean: Place rack between layers of newspaper in a large plastic bag. Saturate the paper with ammonia, close the bag, and let the rack sit overnight. Then rinse with the hose. *Or* lay sheets of aluminum foil over the top of the grill, press down tightly, and place over hot coals for 15 minutes. Remove the foil, and brush off the loosened char. If you brush the grill with vegetable oil, it will be easier to clean next time.

To remove rust: Wipe with a rust retardant/remover, following manufacturer's instructions.

Beads

To clean plastic beads: Place in a pillow case, and wash in washing machine with cold water and cold-water soap. If a bead curtain is especially grimy and sticky, add 1 c vinegar to the final rinse.

Bedsprings

To clean: Vacuum the top, bottom, and sides, using the upholstery-brush attachment of your vacuum cleaner.

To prevent mildew: Spray lightly with a disinfectant spray.

Bicycles

Periodic maintenance checks will help you avoid major repairs. Some bicycle shops give free or low-cost seminars on repair and upkeep, and most dealers are willing to advise you on minor repairs.

To clean: Clean the body and spokes with 1 qt warm water and 1 tbsp ammonia in a spray bottle. Rinse well and dry. Do not use a hose—excess water can damage the ball bearings.

To protect: Polish painted, enameled, and chrome parts with an automobile polish. Wipe a leather seat with saddle soap, a vinyl seat with a mixture of water and liquid detergent.

To remove grease, tar, and rust: Wipe with alcohol *or* cleaning fluid.

To do a routine maintenance check: Make sure that **1.** Wheels are straight and aligned. **2.** Brake cables are whole and not rusted. **3.** All screws are tight. **4.** Pivoting screws are adjusted to have some give in each gear, but not so much that they hit the spokes. **5.** Chain is oiled with household oil.

Bird cages

To clean: Replace floor paper, or—if floor is covered with vinyl—clean with soap and water. Check for sprouted seeds and mold under liner and in the slots that hold the tray. Wash water dish and seed cup in hot, soapy water. Rinse well and dry. Wipe cage inside and out with 1 qt warm water mixed with 1 tbsp vinegar *or* alcohol. Dry in the sun, if possible, *or* wipe with a cloth.

To protect from rust: After cleaning, wipe with a very light coating of mineral oil. Remove all excess oil or it may make your bird ill.

Blankets

Follow manufacturer's instructions whenever possible.

(**Wool and Wool Blends**) *To clean:* In general, have these blankets dry cleaned. However, you can wash them by hand, *or* in the machine (gentle cycle) with cold water and cold-water soap. Add 1 c vinegar to the final rinse to keep the blanket from getting stiff with soap residue. Do not overload the machine. Hang the blanket up to dry in the shade over 2 or more clotheslines. Shake to restore fluffiness. Press the bindings with a warm steam iron.

To repel moths: Store blankets in plastic. Sew a few moth crystals into a small cloth bag. Place this cloth bag in the plastic bag. Seal the plastic bag securely with tape.

(**Synthetics**) *To clean:* Wash blanket in the machine with warm water, a mild detergent, and fabric softener. Tumble dry in a warm—not hot—dryer. Press the bindings with a warm steam iron.

(**Electric**) *To clean:* Do not dry clean an electric blanket—dry-cleaning fluids can damage the wiring. Instead, pin a part of the blanket over the plug to protect it, and wash the blanket in the washing machine, using warm water and mild detergent. Add 1 c vinegar to the final rinse. Do not overload the machine. Do not dry in the dryer—hang in the shade over 2 or more clotheslines. Do not wring or twist. Press the bindings with a warm steam iron. Do not use moth crystals with electric blankets when you store them—they may corrode the wiring.

To prevent electrical problems: Check for a blown fuse or overloaded circuit; pins or metal objects stuck into the cord; or a frayed cord or plug. If necessary, take to an appliance repairman to repair the blanket and control.

Books

Place books loosely on the shelf so that air can circulate around them. Dust the spines regularly with a feather or lamb's-wool duster, or with the brush attachment on your vacuum cleaner. Once or twice a year, give your books a thorough dusting: Check for signs of insects, and wipe the shelves with a damp cloth. Let the shelves dry thoroughly before replacing the books.

(**Leather**) *To clean:* Wipe bindings with a soft cloth dampened with a mild solution of soap flakes and warm water. Wipe off excess soap. Let stand for 24 hours before replacing on the shelf.

Leather-bound books

To protect: Use one of the thick shoe dressings available from a shoe-repair shop, *or* castor oil, *or* lanolin. Do not use mineral oil or petroleum products. Rub the dressing between your hands to warm it, and rub well into the bindings. Let stand for 24 hours, then polish with a soft cloth.

(**Vinyl, Plastic, or Imitation Leather**) *To clean:* Wipe with a solution of warm, soapy water, with a little liquid fabric softener added to prevent static electricity. Let sit until dry, then replace.

(**Cloth**) *To clean:* Rub with an art-gum eraser *or* stale, but still soft, white bread crumbs. Be certain to brush off all the crumbs, or you may attract insects.

To remove stains: Use Opalene, a powdered rubber in a cloth bag (available from art-supply stores).

(**Special Problems**) *Insect damage:* Place small cloth bags filled with a few moth crystals on the back of the shelves. Keep out of the reach of children—the crystals are poisonous. If you suspect that silverfish or other insects are still in the books, shake the books (outdoors) and wipe each page with a cloth that's barely dampened with alcohol.

Mildew: Rub the bindings and affected pages with a soft cloth dampened with alcohol. Then insert sheets of white paper towel between the treated pages, or air the pages for 24 hours.

Stacked china plates

Powdery leather. This is an indication that the leather is deteriorating. Contact a professional book binder.

Small holes or torn pages: Mend with Holland tape (available at an art-supply store), the type used for stamp hinges. Do not use cellophane or any other pressure-sensitive tape—it will damage the paper. If you have a valuable book that you want rebound or repaired, ask your local museum to recommend a reputable bindery.

Wet books: Freeze the books until you have the chance to treat them, then take them to a book restorer. *Or* place them in a microwave oven for 5 to 7 minutes on the lowest setting. Repeat as necessary until they are dry. The only binding that can be damaged by this method is vellum—a light or white skin that will shrink in a microwave. If the book is merely damp, place white paper towels between the pages and on both sides of the binding, weight the book down flat, and leave for 24 hours.

Bottles and vases

To clean and deodorize: Soak overnight in hot water with detergent and ammonia *or* baking soda added. (Do not use ammonia to clean baby bottles). Scrub the inside of bottles with a bottle brush, then rinse well and dry. Clean oily bottles by filling them with sand before scrubbing.

To loosen sediment: Add small stones or tacks to the hot, soapy water, and shake gently.

To remove labels: Soak in hot water until label can be scrubbed off, *or* scrape off with a razor blade. Remove remaining glue with acetone (nail polish remover) or cleaning fluid.

Box springs

See Bedsprings.

Breadbox

To clean: Brush out crumbs. Wipe with hot, soapy water; rinse; and dry.

To deodorize: Wipe with white vinegar.

To remove stains and tarnish from metal: Rub with very fine steel wool *or* emery paper, and cooking oil.

To protect metal from rust: Wipe with a light coating of mineral oil.

Brick

To clean: Scrub with a solution of water and washing soda *or* TSP.

To remove oily stains: Make a paste of TSP and water, apply to stain, and let sit until dry. Brush or scrape off, and rinse well.

To remove soot and smoke: Mix a paste of ammonia and powdered pumice (available at hardware stores). Apply to the stain and allow to dry. Brush or scrape off, wash with hot water and TSP solution, and rinse well.

Brooms

To clean: Swish in hot, soapy water, rinse, and hang up to dry. To restore the broom's shape, wrap rubber bands around the bristles while they are wet.

Brushes

To clean: Wash in hot, soapy water with ammonia *or* baking soda *or* vinegar added. Rinse in warm, then cold, water, and shake. Hang *or* place head-up to dry.

To sterilize hair brushes: Boil in water (if the handle will not be damaged), *or* soak in a disinfectant solution. *See* Crystal, Ivory, or Silver to clean brush handles made of these materials.

Candles

To clean: Wipe with alcohol.

To slow burning and dripping: Freeze for an hour before lighting.

Ceramics

To clean: Swish in hot, soapy water, then rinse and dry. Do not soak unglazed earthenware.

To remove stains: **1.** Rub with a paste of baking soda and water. Use a small brush or Q-tip to get into crevices; *or* **2.** Simmer in a solution of coffee-pot stain remover and water. Do not soak or boil unglazed ceramics; *or* **3.** Rub with vinegar.

Chandeliers

To clean: **1.** Remove crystals and wash them in hot, soapy water with a little ammonia added; *or* **2.** Protect floor or table with drop cloths. Cover light sockets with small plastic bags held in place with rubber bands or twist ties. Spray evenly with a commercial chandelier cleaner. Rinsing is unnecessary; *or* **3.** Protect floor or table with drop cloths. Wear cotton gloves and dip hands in a solution of 1 qt warm water and 1 tbsp ammonia. Wipe each crystal with gloved hands, then rinse and dry with paper towels; *or* **4.** Protect floor and table with drop cloths. Leave crystals in place. Fill a drinking glass with 3 parts warm water and 1 part alcohol. Raise glass to immerse each crystal. Rinsing is not necessary.

China

To clean: Spread a towel in the sink to protect china during washing. Then wash gently in hot, soapy water, with a little vinegar added to cut the grease and add shine. Rinse well and dry with a soft cloth. Do not wash decorated or fine china in the dishwasher—the temperature is too high and the colors may fade.

To remove stains: Rub with a paste of baking soda and water. Do not use abrasive pads or powders, which may scratch china.

To repair small cracks: Boil small pieces in milk (start with cold milk) for 10 minutes. Allow milk to cool before removing china.

To store: Stack china with paper towels *or* plates *or* circles of felt between each piece. Hang cups on plastic-coated hooks. If storing china in a cool cupboard, let it warm up before serving hot foods or liquids.

Cloisonné

To clean: Wash in lukewarm, soapy water, rinse, and dry. Do not soak. Do not use abrasive scouring powders or hot water.

To remove stains: Rub gently with a paste made of baking soda and water.

Combs

To clean: Soak in a solution of water and baking soda *or* ammonia for 15 minutes, then scrub with a brush.

To sterilize: Soak in a disinfectant solution. Nylon combs can also be boiled, but rubber or plastic combs cannot.

Comforters

(**Down**) *To clean:* Wash in washing machine in warm water, a mild detergent, and ½ c of a water softener such as washing soda. Dissolve powders thoroughly in water before adding comforter. Put machine on rinse and spin cycles twice to remove all the detergent and as much water as possible. If the comforter is too large for your washer, wash it in the bathtub, stomping on it with your bare feet as if you were crushing grapes. Rinse repeatedly, then remove as much water as possible by spinning comforter in washing machine. Tumble dry on low heat, or hang over several clotheslines to dry, and shake and fluff frequently.

(**Synthetic Fiber-Filled**) *To clean:* Consult manufacturer's instructions, when possible. Hand washing is the safest method. Your comforter may wash safely in your machine (see Down), or you may want to have it cleaned professionally.

Concrete

To clean: Sponge with a solution of 3 tbsp washing soda *or* TSP to each gallon of water used. Rinse.

To remove stains: Make a paste of water and 3 tbsp washing soda *or* TSP *or* dishwasher soap. Apply to stain and let sit until dry. Then brush off and rinse. If stain remains, mix a solution of oxalic acid (available from paint and hardware stores)

and water. Follow label directions exactly: Oxalic acid is a corrosive poison.

Countertops

(**Butcherblock and Wooden**) *To clean:* Scrape with a plastic scraper, then rub with salt. Rinse well and wipe dry.

To deodorize and disinfect: Scrub with a solution of warm water and chlorine bleach *or* dry baking soda *or* a low-abrasive cleaning powder. Rinse well—under running water, if possible—and dry.

To protect: Rub surfaces used for food with vegetable oil; rub other surfaces with mineral oil. Let sit for 5 to 15 minutes, then wipe up excess oil.

(**Plastic**) *To clean, deodorize, and disinfect:* Scrape with a plastic scraper, then wipe with a paste of baking soda and water. Finally, wipe with equal parts chlorine bleach and water *or* a disinfectant, and rinse well.

Crystal

To clean: Wash in hot, soapy water with a little vinegar added to cut grease. Plain crystal can be washed with a little ammonia added. Don't, however, use ammonia on crystal with decorative trim—it can fade the color.

To remove stains and discoloration: Pour in a solution of sand and alcohol, shake gently, and rinse. *Or* dissolve a denture tablet in hot water, allow to cool, immerse crystal, and soak overnight. Rinse well with vinegar, then with water. Never soak or plunge cold glassware into hot water—it may break.

To smooth rough edges and chips: Rub gently with wet emery paper.

Dishes

For cleaning, *see* individual materials.

Dried flowers

To clean: Shake gently in a paper bag with 1 c cornstarch *or* salt.

Earthenware

See Ceramics.

Feathers

Follow cleaning directions for dried flowers.

Butcherblock countertop

Fiberglass

To clean: Use a commercial fiberglass cleaner *or* a commercial scrubbing foam. Do not use abrasives.

To restore shine and color: Polish the outside with automobile wax.

To repair cracks and chips: Use a commercial fiberglass repair kit (available at hardware stores).

Fish tanks

See Aquariums.

Foam rubber

When cleaning foam-filled cushions or foam mattresses, don't use strong chemicals—they will speed up the deterioration·process and cause the foam to give off a noxious odor. Once the foam has begun to deteriorate, the process cannot be reversed. In this case, replace the foam.

Gilt

To clean and protect: Have cleaned professionally, or wipe gilt very gently with a soft cloth dampened with a solution of 1 qt water and 1 tbsp ammonia *or* vinegar. Protect frequently handled gilt objects with several thin layers of white shellac.

Glass

To clean: Use a commercial window-cleaning solution *or* make a solution of 1 tbsp vinegar *or* ammonia and 1 tbsp alcohol in a pint spray bottle of water. Wipe or spray on the solution, and polish with a soft, lint-free cloth or use a squeegee (see page 79). To clean glass

Kerosene lamp

doorknobs, soak them in 1 qt water and ½ c ammonia.

To remove stains: Rub with a solution of 1 tbsp washing soda *or* TSP dissolved in 1 qt water.

To smooth rough edges: Sand with fine emery paper.

To protect mirror backing: Coat with clear shellac.

To keep from clouding: Rub with glycerine (available at a pharmacy), bar soap *or* glass wax, then wipe off excess.

Horn
To clean and remove stains: Rub with petroleum jelly, olive oil, or boiled linseed oil. Wipe off excess; polish to a shine.

Ivory
To clean: Expose to light as much as possible—ivory darkens in the absence of light.

To remove stains: For stains and discoloration, call in a professional. However, you can try wiping the ivory with equal parts lemon juice and water, *or* apply a paste of lemon juice and whiting (available from a pharmacy). Let paste dry, brush off, and polish with a cloth. Avoid excess water.

Jade
To clean: Rub with a solution of 1 c water and 1 tbsp ammonia, *or* use a commercial jewelry stone cleaner.

Jewelry
(**Diamonds, gold, rubies, and sapphires**) *To clean:* Soak in a solution of 1 c warm water and ¼ c ammonia. Rinse under warm run-

ning water. You can scrub with a soft brush, but do not pick at stones and settings with a sharp object.

(**Gold-filled**) *To clean:* Wipe with a damp cloth.

(**Pearls**) *To clean:* Soak pins or rings in a solution of liquid soap and warm water. Do not soak strings of pearls—wipe them off with the solution. Do not use ammonia on pearls.

(**Silver**) *To clean:* Polish with silver cloth. Store in cornmeal to prevent tarnish.

Kitchen knives
To clean: Wash in hot, soapy water. Do not place wooden handles or hollow-handled silver in the dishwasher—the heat may damage them. Do not soak wooden handles—instead, clean and protect them by rubbing with vegetable oil.

To remove stains and rust: Rub stainless and carbon steel with very fine emery paper and alcohol. Wash and rinse.

To sharpen: Use a blade stone, steel, *or* an electric knife sharpener. *Or* have your good knives sharpened professionally.

To store: Use a rack with individual slots to protect the blades.

Lamps
If you have electrical problems: Check for a faulty bulb, a blown fuse, a tripped circuit breaker, frayed wiring, or a broken plug or switch. You will find lamp-repair techniques discussed in Ortho's book, *Basic Home Repairs.*

(**Bases**) *To clean:* Wipe porcelain and metal bases with a damp cloth, and dry immediately to prevent spots and streaks. Do not immerse the base in water.

To protect: Oil or wax wood, polish chrome, and wipe plastics with furniture oil.

(**Fluorescent Lamps**) Dust regularly. When the bulb begins to darken at one end, turn it around to lengthen its life.

(**Fluorescent Panels**) Remove the panels, and wash in hot, soapy water; then wipe dry. Wipe the bulbs when cool with a damp cloth or sponge, and replace the panels.

(**Light Bulbs**) When they are cool, wipe them with a damp cloth or sponge.

(**Kerosene Lamps**) Wipe the base with hot, soapy water; wipe dry. Clean burners and chimneys in hot, soapy water; rinse and dry. Pinch off—never cut—wicks. If wicks become especially dirty, boil them in water and let them air dry. Apply a little candle wax to the end of the wick to make it easier to insert. For the best light, keep lamp oil ⅔ full.

(**Shades**) A shade's cellophane wrapping will not protect it from dust—the wrapping may shrink and damage the shade. For real protection, dust the shade often, inside and out, with a feather duster.

Acrylic: Wipe with a damp cloth. Use a commercial acrylic cleaner to polish.

Fabric: If the fabric is sewn rather than glued to the frame, and is made of rayon, nylon, or fiberglass, then dip it in warm, soapy water, rinse, and dry outdoors in the shade *or* indoors in front of a fan or window. Dry-clean glued fabric shades, or shades that have glued ornamentation.

Paper: Condition shades made of true parchment once a year with neat's foot oil (available at shoe-repair shops). Clean other paper shades by wiping with a soft cloth dipped in furniture polish. Use an art-gum eraser to remove smudges.

Plastic: Wipe with warm, soapy water; rinse and dry.

Leather
(**Shoes**) *To clean:* Polish with leather cleaner/conditioner. Dry wet shoes at room temperature—excess heat will cause them to harden. Wipe patent leather with petroleum jelly, then wipe off excess. Rub off spots with an art-gum eraser. For difficult stains, consult a shoe repairman.

(**Gloves**) *To clean:* Put gloves on hands, then wash with soap suds. Wipe with a towel. Roll in a towel, and dry flat. Knead to soften.

(**Handbags and Wallets**) *To clean:* Polish with leather cleaner/conditioner. Dry wet bags at room temperature—excess heat will cause them to harden. Wipe with paste wax, and rub to polish. Remove spots with an art-gum eraser.

Mildew: Wipe with alcohol, then apply leather conditioner.

Luggage

See individual material: Aluminum, page 61, Leather and Fabrics, pages 38–41.

Marble

To clean: Use a solution of warm water and a mild detergent *or* washing soda. Rinse and dry.

To polish: Use a commercial marble polish, following label directions. *Or* call in a professional.

To remove stains: Wipe with hydrogen peroxide. Rinse well. For deep stains, apply a paste of hydrogen peroxide and whiting (available at a pharmacy). Allow to dry, then brush off. Rinse and polish. Avoid acids such as vinegar.

Marcasite

To clean: An ornament of this material is probably an antique. Have it cleaned by a professional antique restorer.

Mats

(**Fabric**) *To clean:* Wash rubber- and fiber-backed fabric mats by hand in cold-water soap. For unbacked cotton, wool, and synthetics, see Fabric section, pages 38–41.

(**Fiber**) *To clean:* Shake or sweep coconut, jute, or hemp mats on both sides to avoid damaging the floor underneath. Wash heavily soiled fiber mats with mild detergent and water, using a brush or broom. Rinse with a hose or under a running faucet, and lay flat to dry.

(**Plastic**) *To clean:* Wipe with detergent and warm water, then rinse and dry.

(**Rubber**) *To clean:* Wash in detergent and warm water, in washing machine *or* by hand. Avoid chlorine bleach; however, you can use it occasionally to remove mildew and treat stains. Do not dry in a gas or electric dryer—wipe or air dry, instead.

Mattresses

Turn regularly to distribute wear.

To freshen: Air outdoors if possible, or indoors with the windows open and a fan running. Spray lightly with disinfectant before airing to retard mildew growth.

To protect: Use a mattress pad or dust cover. Wash the pad or cover every two or three months.

To remove stains: Follow the guidelines for cleaning upholstery in the Stain chart, pages 42–51.

Mirrors

To clean: Use a commercial window cleaner, *or* 1 tbsp ammonia *or* alcohol in a pint spray bottle filled with water. Be careful not to spill any of the liquid on the silver backing—water and chemicals will cause it to darken.

To prevent steamy glass: Rub with bar soap *or* glass wax *or* a little glycerine, and polish.

To repair silver backing: As a temporary measure, tape a piece of aluminum foil to the back of the mirror. For a more permanent remedy, have a glass-replacement firm replace the silver backing. To protect new backing, brush with several coats of white shellac.

Mops

(**Dust**) Shake outdoors, or into a paper bag, after each use. If the head can be removed, wash it in the washing machine with a mild detergent and warm water. Add 1 c vinegar to final rinse. Shake to untangle, and air dry. If the head cannot be removed, wash it in a sink or tub with detergent and warm water. Wring, shake, and air dry. To wash oiled mops that have become grimy, add ½ c ammonia to the wash cycle, and 1 c vinegar to the final rinse. Hang dry, and oil again. Trim loose fibers and frayed ends.

(**Rag**) Rinse well after each use, and wash as for dust mops.

(**Sponge**) Freshen and deodorize by rinsing in a mild chlorine-bleach solution. Rinse well, and air dry before storing.

Mother-of-pearl

To clean: Wash, but do not soak, in a mild solution of lukewarm water and detergent. Rinse, then dry. Do not use ammonia or abrasives. Do not wash in dishwasher.

Leather accessories

Onyx

To clean: Wash in hot, soapy water. Rinse, then dry.

Paint brushes and rollers

(**Latex**) Rinse immediately after use until water is clear. Wash with detergent and warm water, rinse, and shake out excess water. Hang to dry. (**Oil and Acrylic**) Rinse or soak in paint thinner or turpentine. Sprinkle with dry laundry detergent, working it into the bristles or nap. Rinse well under warm running water until water is clear, shake, and hang to dry. You can buy a device at hardware stores for spinning the water out of brushes and rollers.

Paintings and prints

To clean or restore valuable works of art, take to a professional art restorer. Ask your local museum or art gallery for recommendations. For light cleaning, dust the surface gently with a lamb's-wool duster.

Papier-mâché

To clean: Wipe with a damp sponge. While papier-mâché is still damp, sprinkle with white flour. When it is dry, polish with a soft cloth. Avoid hot water.

Phonograph records

To clean: Wipe with a commercial antistatic cleaner for records *or* a mild detergent solution. Rinse and dry thoroughly. Always wipe *with* the grooves, to avoid scratching the record. If the playing arm does not have a dust brush, wipe records each time you play them to avoid scratches.

Copper sauté pan

To restore a warped record: Place between two sheets of glass, and leave in the sun until flat.

Photographs
To clean: Rub with slightly stale, soft-white-bread crumbs.

To flatten: Dip photographs in a commercial flattening solution (available from camera shops), *or* press flat between two sheets of paper.

Pianos
Pianos are easily affected by temperature, moisture, and pressure changes. Place them in rooms where the temperature and humidity remain as constant as possible, away from sunlight, windows, and heat sources. Because they are sensitive, they need to be tuned, regulated, and cleaned by a professional on a regular basis, preferably with each change of season. Commercial piano humidity regulators are available from piano stores.

To clean: Treat the case as a piece of fine furniture. (*See* page 34.) Wipe the keyboard regularly with a damp cloth, then dry immediately to avoid damage to keys. To keep ivory from yellowing, expose the keyboard to light. Wipe plastic keys with an all-purpose cleaner. Rinse and dry. Don't let liquids drip between the keys.

(**Special Problems**) *Moths in wool hammers:* Tape a small cloth bag of camphor or moth crystals inside the piano case.

Yellowing ivory: You can try restoring yellowed ivory with a solution of equal parts lemon juice and water. *Or,* if you don't want to take the risk, have the ivory bleached professionally.

Pillows
To freshen: Tumble in a clothes dryer for half an hour along with several slightly damp, clean, terrycloth towels and a sheet of fabric softener.

(**Down and Polyester Fiber-Filled**) Wash by hand or machine with mild detergent and warm water. Add 1 c vinegar to final rinse to remove all the detergent. Dry in warm (not hot) clothes dryer, *or* outdoors—shake to fluff up the filling. If you don't mind the smell, spray lightly with a disinfectant spray before drying to deodorize and prevent mildew.

(**Kapok and Foam Rubber**) Take to a professional cleaner or laundry.

Plaster of paris
To clean: Apply a paste of laundry starch and hot water to the object. Allow to dry, then brush off.

To restore: Spray with several thin coats of white latex paint. Allow each coat to dry between layers.

Plastics
To clean: Wash in warm, soapy water. In washing machines, wash plastic bags, shower curtains, and baby bibs on the shortest cycle, using detergent, water softener, and warm water. Air dry in the shade.

To sanitize and deodorize: Add ½ c chlorine bleach to the wash cycle or cleaning solution. Add ½ c baking soda to the rinse water. Avoid abrasives, heat, alcohol, and acetone (nail polish remover).

Plastic laminates
To clean: Sponge with hot, soapy water.

To remove stains: Scrub with dry dishwasher detergent or baking soda, *or* use a commercial plastic laminate cleaner (available from paint stores). Avoid abrasives, such as scouring pads and powders—they will eventually break down the surface.

To bleach: Flood with a solution of equal parts chlorine bleach and water. Let sit for about 10 minutes, then rinse well. Follow with a baking-soda solution to remove the strong chlorine odor.

Porcelain
To clean: Wash in warm, soapy water. Use an artist's paint brush or a Q-tip to clean hard-to-reach places.

To remove stains: Use acetone (nail polish remover) *or* alcohol. Rinse well, pat dry with paper towels, and allow to air-dry thoroughly.

Porcelain enamel
To clean: Wash with an all-purpose household cleaner *or* liquid detergent, and hot water. Do not use abrasives, except for a low-abrasive cleansing powder.

To remove stains: Use a low-abrasive cleansing powder. Scrub rusty-water stains, medicine dyes, and mildew with chlorine bleach, *or* a paste of TSP and water, *or* a paste of cream of tartar and hydrogen peroxide, *or* a commercial porcelain rust-remover and cleaner.

To repair chips or gouges: Use a commercial porcelain enamel paint (available at a hardware or paint store).

To remove decals: Soak in laundry pre-wash product for an hour, *or* spray with hair spray. Then scrape off decals with a plastic spatula.

Pots and pans
(**Aluminum**) Wash by hand, not in dishwasher—the detergent may discolor pots and pans. Use a soft scrubber. Don't use scouring powder. To loosen scorched food, soak pots and pans in hot water and detergent, or boil with equal parts vinegar and water. To eliminate discoloration, cook acid foods—for example, tomatoes and vinegar—in the pot. To loosen mineral deposits in kettles, boil equal parts vinegar and water. Do not use abrasive scouring pads or powders on non-stick or mirror-finish aluminum.

(**Cast Iron**) To season new cast iron cookware, scour off any lacquer coating, wash in hot, soapy water, and coat the inside with cooking oil or solid shortening. Heat in a 325°F oven for several hours, reoiling as necessary. Wipe off excess oil; rinse before using. Do not store food in cast iron, especially acid foods such as tomatoes.

To clean: Rub with salt, then rinse and dry—preferably in a warm oven. Recoat with cooking oil. Remove rust with fine steel wool, then reseason.

(**Copper**) Wash in mild detergent and warm water. Polish with copper polish, then rinse and dry quickly to avoid water spots. Remove verdigris (green oxidation) immediately—it is toxic. Do so by scrubbing with a solution of 1 qt water and 1 tsp ammonia. *Or* boil equal parts vinegar, salt, and water. Avoid abrasive scouring pads and powders.

(**Enamelware**) Wash in hot, soapy water. Rub stains with a paste of baking soda and water. To lengthen the life of new pans, boil water for 15 minutes. Don't store acid foods, such as tomatoes, in enamelware. Allow pot to cool before washing, and avoid sudden temperature changes. Don't use very chipped pots and pans.

(**Non-Stick Finishes**) Use non-metal utensils to keep from damaging the surface. Wash with hot, soapy water. Avoid abrasive scouring pads and powders. Soak in hot water to remove stains and burned-on food. The finish will last longer if you wash this cookware by hand rather than in the dishwasher.

(**Stainless Steel**) Wash in hot, soapy water, rinse, then dry quickly to avoid water spots. Remove stains with vinegar or silver polish. Do not use abrasive scouring pads or powders—they will scratch the cookware's surface, and thus be harder to keep clean. Excessively salty or acidic foods may discolor stainless steel.

Racquets

To protect wooden handles: Wipe with furniture oil, *or* spray with varnish or shellac.

To restring tennis racquets: Take to a sporting goods or tennis shop.

Razors

(**Non-Electric**) Soak in a solution of water and a dissolved denture tablet.

(**Electric**) If the head can be removed, wash it in hot, soapy water. If not, brush the head with a stiff brush.

Rubber

To clean: Scrub with a solution of ½ gal hot water, and 1 tbsp ammonia *or* alcohol, and liquid detergent. *Or* place in an almost-full load of laundry in washing machine, adding 1 tbsp bleach *or* ½ c ammonia to wash cycle. Hang up to air dry.

To store: Wrap hot-water bottles in newspapers, and place in a cool, dry place. Avoid heat, light, and cleaning solvents.

Shower curtains

To clean: Wash by hand using warm water and a mild detergent, *or* in the machine on the gentlest cycle. Hang to dry.

To remove mildew: Add ½ c chlorine bleach to the wash, *or* spray with disinfectant.

Smoke detectors

Accumulated dust and atmospheric oils will eventually hinder the effectiveness of your smoke detector. Vacuum around it once a month. Test according to manufacturer's directions, or by holding a lighted pipe or cigarette towards the unit. Replace batteries when necessary.

Sponges

To clean, sanitize, and deodorize: Wash sponges in the washing machine when bleaching a load of laundry, *or* put in the dishwasher. *Or* boil in salt water for 5 minutes.

Synthetic marble

To clean: Wipe with hot, soapy water.

To remove stains and scratches: Rub gently with baking soda, dishwasher detergent, or a low-abrasive scouring cleanser.

To restore shine: Rub with a commercial rubbing compound made especially for synthetic marble (available at hardware stores).

Tea kettles

To clean: Clean according to the

Tea kettle

material—copper, porcelain, enamel, and so on.

To remove mineral deposits: Boil water and a commercial coffee-pot cleaner *or* ½ c vinegar in the kettle for 15 minutes. Leave overnight, and rinse well.

Thermos bottles

To clean and deodorize: Rinse out contents with hot water as soon as possible. Fill bottle with hot water and baking soda, let it soak overnight, then scrub with a bottle brush. Rinse.

Toilets

To clean: Use sudsy water or an all-purpose cleaner. If using a commercial toilet bowl cleaner, do not mix with any other chemicals, especially chlorine—some combinations can produce toxic gases. You can use chlorine bleach by itself to clean, disinfect, and deodorize toilet bowls, but pour it in carefully to avoid splashing on you and your clothes.

To remove rust stains: Use a commercial rust-remover according to manufacturer's directions.

To deodorize: To prevent odors, clean regularly with a disinfectant cleaner or chlorine bleach. Be aware that commercial in-bowl or tank cleaner/deodorizers are mainly a perfume, and may contain toxic chemicals.

Tortoise shell

To clean: Wash with mild detergent and water. Rinse well and dry thoroughly.

Mini blinds

To protect: Polish with a furniture polish.

Tubs, showers, and sinks

(**Ceramic Tile**) *To clean:* Use a commercial scrubbing foam, disinfectant cleaner, washing soda, TSP, or ammonia and water.

To remove stains: Make a paste of TSP or washing soda and water, and tape onto the spot. Leave for several hours, rewetting when necessary. Rub with vinegar to remove the cleaner and restore the shine.

To clean grout: Use a stiff brush and scouring powder.

To remove mineral deposits: Wipe with vinegar, or equal parts ammonia and water, then rinse.

To remove mildew: Spray with commercial mildew remover or a chlorine bleach solution. Then wipe with a solution of baking soda and water to remove the chlorine odor.

To repair chips and cracks: See Ortho's book, *Basic Home Repairs.*
(**Fiberglass**) *To clean:* Use a commercial fiberglass cleaner or commercial scrubbing foam. Do not use abrasives.

To restore the shine and color: Polish the outside of the tub or shower with automobile wax. Do not use abrasive scouring pads or powders.

To repair cracks and chips: Use a commercial fiberglass repair kit (available at hardware stores).
(**Glass**) *To clean and remove mineral deposits and soap scum:* Wipe

with vinegar or equal parts ammonia and water.
(**Porcelain Enamel**) *To clean:* Clean with a mildly abrasive scrubbing powder or with an all-purpose cleaner. Leave it on for half an hour to let the chemical work, then rinse.

To bleach, disinfect, and remove yellowing: Use a solution of chlorine bleach and water. To clean a sink, fill it with water and add 1 c chlorine bleach. Let sit for half an hour. Rinse, then wipe with baking soda to remove chlorine odor.

To remove rust, mineral deposits, and other stains: Rub with a paste of cream of tartar (available at grocery stores), and hydrogen peroxide. Leave on for an hour or two, then rinse. Do not use abrasive scouring pads or powders—they scratch the surface, making it more difficult to keep clean. Try dry dishwasher detergent instead.

To remove decals: Spray or sponge with a laundry pre-wash product. Leave this on for an hour, then scrape up decals with a plastic spatula.

To repair chips or deep scratches: Use a commercial porcelain-enamel repair compound (available at paint and hardware stores).

To remove burned-on food: Cover with a wet, soapy cloth. Leave on for an hour, then scrape off excess with a plastic spatula, and rinse.
(**Stainless Steel**) *To clean:* Wash with hot, soapy water, and dry to avoid spots. Polish the outside with a thin coat of mineral oil or silver polish.

To remove stains: Rub with a mildly abrasive cleanser, then with vinegar to remove soap film. Avoid strong alkaline cleaners such as washing soda, which will darken the metal, and abrasives such as scouring powder.

Typewriter

Periodic cleaning and oiling: Clean and condition the small paper rollers and the large roller by wiping them with alcohol. Remove the large roller bar, if possible, and vacuum or blot out the dust underneath. Move the roller bar to the far right, and place a drop of typewriter or sewing machine oil on the

rails. Clean the type with a commercial type-cleaner or a soft art-gum eraser. When the typewriter is not in use, protect it with a cover or store it in its case.

Umbrellas

To remove mildew: Sponge with alcohol.

Vases

To clean: Clean as for bottles, page 54.

To remove plant stains: Fill with hot, soapy water and vinegar or a denture tablet, and leave overnight. Add uncooked rice or marbles, and shake until sediment is loosened. Then rinse well.

Venetian and mini blinds

To clean: Wipe both sides of each slat with an all-purpose cleaner or baking-soda-and-water solution. Or use a commercial venetian blind cleaner (does not require rinsing). Scrub the tapes with a soft brush and warm, soapy water, then rinse. You can wash smaller mini blinds in the shower or tub. Dry metal parts with a hair dryer, and coat with mineral oil to prevent rust.

Window shades

(**Plastic and Plastic-Coated Fabric**) *To clean:* Remove from window and lay flat. Scrub both sides with hot water and an all-purpose cleaner. Sponge to rinse, then dry. Roll up at once to flatten, then unroll and air dry before rolling up. Spot clean with an art-gum eraser.
(**Fabric**) *To clean:* Take to a professional dry cleaner.

To tighten or loosen roller mechanism: Adjust the spring at the end of the roller—clockwise to tighten, counterclockwise to loosen.

Woodenware

Clean as for wooden countertops, page 54.

To season: Wipe with cooking oil. Do not place in dishwasher. Avoid abrasive scouring pads and cleansers.

METALS

Use this chart to select appropriate metal cleaners and to find out how to restore tarnished and stained metals. The key to keeping metals looking their best is cleaning them regularly so that tarnish and stains don't build up.

Metal	To Polish	To Remove Stains	Cautions and Comments
Aluminum	Use an aluminum or copper cleaner.	Simmer with equal parts vinegar and water. If stain remains, rub with paste of cream of tartar and lemon juice, using a soft scouring pad.	Avoid abrasive scouring pads and powders. Avoid strong alkalis such as washing soda. Do not store food in aluminum.
Brass	Use a brass or copper cleaner. Clean small objects by boiling in equal parts vinegar and water.	Rub with paste of lemon juice *or* vinegar, and salt. Remove lacquer with alcohol *or* acetone (nail polish remover).	Avoid abrasive scouring pads and powders.
Bronze	Rub with boiled linseed oil.	Verdigris: Scrub with vinegar *or* turpentine, using a soft brush.	Avoid abrasive scouring pads and powders.
Chrome	Use silver polish. Rinse, and dry immediately to avoid water spots.	Rub with baking soda and alcohol paste *or* ammonia.	Avoid abrasive scouring pads and powders, harsh metal cleaners and salt, and acids such as vinegar.
Copper	Use a copper cleaner.	Verdigris: Use solution of 1 qt water and 1 tsp ammonia, *or* boil in 1 qt water with ½ c each salt and vinegar.	Remove verdigris from cooking utensils—it is toxic. Avoid abrasive scouring pads and powders.
Gold	Wipe or soak in ½ c warm water and 1 tsp ammonia.		Avoid abrasive scouring pads and powders, and harsh metal cleaners.
Iron	Rub with salt, rinse, and dry. Season with cooking oil before storing.	Rub with fine steel wool and cooking oil. Protect items not used for cooking with a rust retardant.	Avoid acids such as vinegar or tomatoes. Do not store food in iron cooking pots and pans.
Lead	Wipe with turpentine.	Boil in several changes of water. Scrub with turpentine.	Lead is poisonous and should never be used for cooking or storing food.
Nickel	Wipe with alcohol or any metal polish.	Scrub with paste of salt and alcohol.	Nickel will darken unless cleaned frequently.
Pewter	Clean and polish with paste of cooking oil and rottenstone (available from a pharmacy).	Use a commercial pewter cleaner. Remove brown scales by immersing in lye bath for 15 minutes. Scrub with a brush, and rinse well. See page 13 for cautions regarding lye.	Avoid abrasive scouring pads and powders.
Silver	Use silver polish. Rinse and dry quickly to avoid water spots. Store in plastic wrap or anti-tarnish silver cloth to avoid spots and tarnish.	Use silver polish to remove most stains and tarnish.	Eggs, salt, harsh abrasives, and some sauces will tarnish silver. Do not put hollow-handled knives in the dishwasher. Rubber bands or gloves will darken silver.
Stainless steel	Wash with hot soapy water and dry quickly to avoid water spots. Polish with silver polish.	Rub with vinegar. Mildly abrasive cleaners can be used on textured surfaces. Protect surfaces not used for food with mineral oil. Restaurant cooks wipe their stainless steel surfaces with hot coffee—the oils leave a protective finish.	Avoid alkalis such as washing soda, harsh metal cleaners, and abrasive scouring pads and powders.
Tin	Wash with warm soapy water, and dry quickly to avoid water spots and rust.	Remove rust with fine steel wool and cooking oil. To prevent rust, wipe surfaces not used for food with mineral oil.	Tin baking pans heat better and bake more evenly when they are allowed to darken.
Wrought iron	Polish with liquid wax or polish.	Remove rust with kerosene and fine steel wool *or* emery paper. Protect from rust with a solvent-based floor wax, *or* paint with a rust-inhibiting paint especially for metal.	Paint outdoor furniture with a rust-inhibiting paint made especially for metal.
Zinc	Wash in soapy water and dry quickly to prevent water spots.	Rub with vinegar *or* lemon juice; *or* scrub with a mildly abrasive cleanser.	Avoid abrasive scouring pads and powders.

APPLIANCES

Gas stove

Keep your owner's manual handy—familiarize yourself with which parts can be removed for cleaning, and how to use the appliances properly. If you can't locate the owner's manual, check the reference section of your library or local appliance dealer, or contact the manufacturer. The box on page 96 lists some major manufacturers of appliances.

Check for the following before calling a repairman:

Electric appliances
1. Are fuses or circuits burnt out, breaker switch thrown?
2. Are cords frayed, plugs or outlets damaged?
3. Is there a reset switch to be pushed?

Gas appliances
1. Are outlet holes blocked?
2. Is copper tubing blocked or damaged? (Open a window and call a repairman or the fire department if you smell *any* leaking gas.)
3. Is the pilot light out?

Plumbing
1. Is a hose or pipe blocked, bent, or damaged?
2. Is the drain plugged?

When you do decide to call, select a repairman with whom you—or a friend—are familiar, or one who advertises service for your brand of appliance. Check your owner's manual and warranty information, if you have it. Ask the repairman for a cost estimate. Offer the following information:

1. Serial and model numbers. (Look for the name plate on the appliance.)
2. Description of unusual noises.
3. Age of the appliance.
4. Description of the repairs you have already attempted.

Large appliances
Keeping your large appliances clean will increase their efficiency and cut down on repairs. Common problems that are easy to check or remedy are included below.

Dishwashers
You may actually save money and energy by using a dishwasher. Washing dishes by hand in constantly running hot water may use up to 60 gallons of water, plus the energy used by the hot-water heater. Most dishwashers use between 10 and 20 gallons for a full load. Check the thermostat—the water should reach 120° to 140° in order to clean and sanitize your dishes properly.

To clean: A dishwasher's interior is self-cleaning, but you may need to remove accumulated food particles from the drain screen and to clean the water jets on the sprayer with a wire. It is normal to have standing water around the drain. Add ½ c baking soda to clean and deodorize the drain.

To unclog: Sprinkle 1 c washing soda close to the drain, and pour in a kettle full of boiling water. Wait an hour or so, then run the empty machine through a cycle. If it remains clogged, call a repairman. Do not use commercial drain cleaners—the lye will corrode aluminum and rubber parts.

To stop overflows: Turn off the shutoff valve, which may be located under the sink. If it isn't, shut off the hot water at the hot-water heater main or outside shut-off (see pages 84–85). Check for food particles in the drain or air gap (on the sink top) and clean out.

Clothes dryers
To clean: Clean the lint screen after each use—accumulated lint decreases the machine's efficiency and is a possible fire hazard. Check the duct pipes occasionally—make certain they are unobstructed and unkinked.

To fix cause of torn laundry: Look for a foreign object lodged in the drum. Sand rough spots with fine emery cloth. Do not use anti-static sprays in the dryer—they may clog the filter.

Freezers
To clean: Temporarily store food in the refrigerator or ice chests. Turn control to "off" or unplug freezer. Remove ice with hot water and a soft spatula. Keep water mopped up. Never use an electric heater—it will damage finish, gaskets, and plastic parts. Wipe the inside of the freezer with a solution of baking soda and water. Then wipe with alcohol *or* vinegar to keep the freezer's contents from sticking.

To adjust temperature: Home freezers should be kept at 0°F. Test by inserting a thermometer between two frozen packages and leaving for 24 hours. If it is warmer or colder than 0°F, adjust the thermostat, leave another 24 hours, and check again. Continue until the ideal temperature is reached.

To care for frostless fan freezer: Make sure that food containers do not interfere with the air flow. Periodically, clean the condenser underneath the freezer compartment. Unplug the freezer, remove the grill in front, and clean the coils with a special brush, available at most appliance stores.

To deal with freezer breakdown: Keep the door closed. Pack dry ice on top of the frozen food. If meat, fish, or poultry have reached room temperature, discard them. Food with ice crystals in the center can be refrozen.

Refrigerators
To clean: Unplug refrigerator, and wipe the inside with a solution of baking soda and water. Remove the drain plug, if there is one, and clean out with baking soda and paper towels. Wipe mineral oil on the door gaskets to keep them from cracking. Clean the condenser coils at the

back or underneath with a refrigerator brush or vacuum—dusty coils will greatly reduce the energy efficiency of your refrigerator. To clean the burner compartment of gas refrigerators, see the manufacturer's instructions. Clean the outside of the refrigerator with an all-purpose cleaner.

To prevent odors: Place a box or bowl of dry baking soda or crushed charcoal on a shelf inside the refrigerator.

To adjust temperature: The ideal temperature is between 36°F and 39°F. To test, place a thermometer in a glass of water that has been in the refrigerator for 12 hours. Check your manual—some refrigerator-freezers have a vent connecting the compartments, which can be adjusted for more or less cold.

To prevent mildew: Wipe the inside with vinegar.

To defrost: Turn the control to defrost, and wait 8 hours *or* place a pan of boiling hot water inside and leave for 1 hour. Sponge out water, scrape out ice with a plastic scraper, and clean with a solution of baking soda and water. (Wipe with alcohol to prevent freezer's contents from sticking.)

Stoves and cooktops

Whether your stove or cooktop is gas or electric, use these guidelines to save energy and prevent damage to the unit.

1. To avoid heat waste and burner damage, use cooking utensils that are the same size as the burners. The flatter the burners are, the better they will heat.
2. Put utensils on burners before turning burners on; Shut burners off before removing utensils.
3. Make sure foil burner liners don't block vent openings.
4. Do not drag utensils across the surface.
5. Wipe up spills immediately, especially from acid foods such as tomatoes and vinegar.

To clean: Use an all-purpose cleaner, not abrasive scouring powders. Do not use a strong alkaline, such as ammonia or washing soda on aluminum parts—it will cause the aluminum to darken.

To remove stains: Scrub porcelain enamel with baking soda, avoiding aluminum parts. Soak gas burners in hot, soapy water, then clean out clogged flame outlets with a wire.

To clean cast iron: See Metals, page 61.

To clean aluminum gas burners: Soak in warm, soapy water overnight, then scrub with a stiff brush.

Ovens

To clean: In electric ovens, place a bowl of ammonia in the oven overnight (do not place ammonia in gas ovens—it may ignite). Then wipe with a soft scrubbing pad. *Or* use a commercial oven cleaner, following manufacturer's directions. Avoid getting oven cleaners on electrical elements.

To loosen encrusted food: In electric ovens, dampen a cloth with ammonia and place it on the spot for about 30 minutes, then wipe off, *or* try scrubbing with dry dishwasher detergent. Do *not* use ammonia in gas ovens—scrub with a mildly abrasive cleanser.

To clean self-cleaning ovens: There are two types—pyrolytic and catalytic. Pyrolytic ovens clean themselves during a special cleaning cycle that raises the temperature to 900°–1000°F, in order to burn off deposits. Do not clean greasy pans this way, however—the grease may generate more smoke than the system can handle. Ash deposits are normal at the end of the cycle, and are easily wiped up. The catalytic cleaning process begins automatically whenever the oven is turned on. The walls have a special finish that helps oxidize deposits to water and carbon dioxide as spills occur. Clean the bottom of the oven by hand. Scrub with dry dishwasher soap, ammonia (electric only), *or* washing soda, using a soft scrubbing pad. Avoid abrasive scrubbing powders, and steel wool.

To prevent spills: Place a small sheet of aluminum foil underneath pies and casseroles (*not* on the bottom, where it may interfere with the heating cycle).

To make oven repairs: See Ortho's book, *Basic Home Repairs.*

Microwave ovens

For general safety precautions, follow these guidelines:

1. Make certain that louvers or air vents are kept unblocked. If your microwave is under a shelf, allow at least 1 inch clearance.
3. If the door gasket or lock mechanism becomes damaged, have it repaired immediately to avoid exposure to radiation. Do not use the oven until it is repaired.
4. Do not use metal of any sort in a microwave oven—it could cause an electric arc and damage to the interior. Use only pans and racks made especially for microwaves.
5. Never try to repair a microwave oven yourself—call a professional.

To clean: Cover spills with a damp paper towel, turn the oven on high for 10 seconds, and wipe when cool. Do not use abrasive scrubbing powders or ammonia.

Convection ovens

Some are self-cleaning. Check the control knobs for this feature. Otherwise, clean the same as you would a regular oven.

Washing machines

To clean: Wipe frequently around the rim and empty the lint trap often. Clean the inside of the machine only after using dyes or a very strong chemical. Then, in the hottest water possible, run the machine through a cycle without laundry, adding ½ c detergent and ½ c chlorine bleach.

To recover lost objects: To remove the agitator, consult your owner's manual or call an appliance repairman for instructions.

To repair a machine that does not fill: Check to make sure that water faucets are open, and that hoses aren't clogged or kinked.

To repair a machine that does not spin: Check to make sure that load is in balance and that machine is not overloaded. Make certain that water is draining properly, and that the drive belt is tightened and in place. See your owner's manual.

To repair a machine that vibrates: Check to make sure that machine is level and not overloaded.

To repair a machine that leaks: Check for worn or kinked hoses, and worn washers.

Small appliances

When small appliances work properly, they are a major household convenience. To keep them in good condition, follow the guidelines below.

Blenders

To clean: Fill blender with water and a drop of liquid detergent, and run for several minutes. Rinse and then dry. Wipe base with an all-purpose cleaner. Do not get water inside base.

To eliminate excessive noise: Remove base plate and check fan blades—they may be bent or broken. Check for loose parts. Check blade assembly and seal for wear, and replace if necessary.

Fans

To clean: Unplug, and remove blades if possible. Wash in hot, soapy water, then rinse and dry before replacing. *Or* clean in place—but don't drip water on moving parts.

To oil: Follow manufacturer's instructions.

To eliminate excessive noise: Oil, tighten bolts, and lubricate bearings. If the housing is plastic, put a drop of glue on loose connections.

Food processors

To repair scratched basket: Rub with acrylic cleanser (available from hardware stores).

To eliminate excessive noise or vibration: Check for food lodged under blade—basket may be overloaded. Check for damaged or missing feet.

To repair leaks: Check to make sure that the bowl is not overloaded, cracked, or set insecurely into socket.

Garbage disposals

To clean and unclog: Grind up the peel of an orange or lemon with hot, running water, *or* ice cubes sprinkled with scouring powder without water. Do not use drain cleaners—the lye could splash up onto your eyes or skin, and it will damage the rubber and plastic parts of your disposal.

To repair jams: Turn off disposal and let it cool. Press reverse button, if there is one (it generally is located underneath the disposal). Otherwise, use the end of a broom handle to manually force the blades into reverse. Grind ice cubes sprinkled with scouring powder without running water.

To restart: Push restart button (usually located underneath the disposal).

To encourage faster draining: Run with hottest water and ½ c washing soda, vinegar, *or* ammonia.

Irons

To remove mineral deposits: Fill with equal parts vinegar and water, turn on high, and steam on rack in sink for a few minutes. Fill again with vinegar and water, let sit for an hour, empty, and rinse with cold water.

To remove stains on plate: Wipe warm iron with vinegar and salt. Run over waxed paper a few times, then wipe off excess wax. *Or* wipe with acetone (nail polish remover).

To prevent mineral deposits: Use distilled water only.

To clear clogged steam vents: When iron is cool, poke out residue with a stiff wire. Use a pipe cleaner to clear spray nozzle.

Mixers

To get beaters to turn: Lubricate according to manufacturer's instructions, and oil in oil ports. Check for worn gears and for loose or bent beater shafts.

To get beater to operate at more than one speed: Turn quickly from low to high. Repeat until control plate contacts are not welded together.

Blender

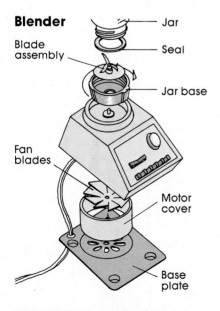

Jar
Seal
Jar base
Blade assembly
Jar base
Fan blades
Motor cover
Base plate

Always consult the manufacturer's manual before repairing any small appliance. If you've lost your manual, write to the manufacturer for a replacement. (See page 96 for addresses.) Not all small appliances can be taken apart, but if you disassemble an appliance, be sure to unplug it first, and keep track of the parts for reassembly. Many appliances have small red dots next to the oil ports (inside or out) to show you where to oil—one or two drops in each port. To clean dirt from fan blades or cooling fins, use a small, dry, stiff artist's brush. Unless the problem is obvious and easily repaired, take the appliance to a professional.

Mixer

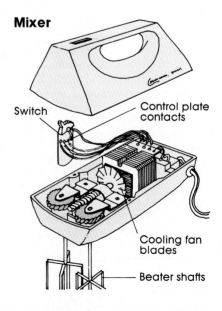

Switch
Control plate contacts
Cooling fan blades
Beater shafts

To eliminate excessive noise or vibration: Check to make sure that beaters do not hit bowl, and that beater shafts are straight. Open case and check to make certain that cooling fan blades are not bent.

Sewing machines

To clean and lubricate: Vacuum or brush out lint and dust around the motor, bobbin case, and all moving parts. Lubricate visible oil ports once a year or more. Use sewing machine oil (available at fabric stores).

To protect: Keep in a closed cabinet, cupboard, or case, *or* cover with a cloth when not in use.

To repair a machine that operates slowly or not at all: Check hand wheel, and tighten clutch if necessary. Adjust tension disk, check controls, and lubricate.

To eliminate excessive noise: Check for loose needle plate and loose wires. Lubricate. Adjust drive belt.

To ease a machine that operates stiffly: The wrong lubricant may have been used. Pour drops of alcohol in oil ports, operate for several minutes, and relubricate with sewing machine oil.

To repair bobbin winder: Check for a worn drive belt or a worn rubber rim on the bobbin winder.

To get fabric to feed: Adjust the pressure foot. Check needle size, bobbin and thread tension, and clogged or loose feeder.

Toasters

To clean: Unplug, remove crumb tray if possible, shake, and gently brush out crumbs with a soft brush. Avoid damaging heating coil. Clean outside with hot, soapy water, then polish dry.

To repair a toaster that overtoasts or undertoasts: Check the inside for stains (which may be giving the wrong message to the thermostat), and clean, if necessary, with baking soda. Adjust thermostat and release spring according to owner's manual.

Trash compactors

To clean: To minimize the need for cleaning, wrap wet garbage in newspapers, and avoid putting in foods with strong odors, such as fish. Remove the ram according to manufacturer's directions, and wash in hot, soapy water. To remove odors, spray compactor and garbage with disinfectant spray.

To get compactor to start: Check to make sure that start button has been pushed, that machine is tightly closed, and that latch is secure. Check to see whether garbage has fallen behind or under the bin.

To eliminate excessive noise: Lubricate according to manufacturer's instructions. Check drive belt for too much slack, and adjust.

Vacuum cleaners

To clean: Change disposable bags frequently—a full bag greatly reduces effectiveness. Clean a cloth bag by shaking it into a large plastic garbage bag, rubbing the bag against itself to loosen embedded dirt. *Or* hang the bag outside and beat out the dust with a stick or carpet beater. Remove the roller brush, and clean off. Empty the cannister of water-filtering vacuums after each use, and wash.

To cool a vacuum that operates hot: Check for clogged hose, dust bag, or exhaust port.

To increase suction: Check for: clogged hose, bag, or exhaust port; loose connections; clogged intake filter; loose fan or drive belt; or disconnected attachments.

To get roller brush to rotate: Check for loose or broken drive belt. Remove hair or thread around roller brush.

To make vacuum easier to push: Reset height adjustment pedal. Check for loose roller brush. Lubricate roller brush with machine oil.

To eliminate excessive noise: Check for loose objects in hose or housing. Check for loose or bent fan.

Cannister Vacuum

To clear a clogged hose, either reverse it, holding the hose against the intake port so that the suction pulls stuck objects through, or remove the hose from the vacuum, and push the clog out with a wire hanger.

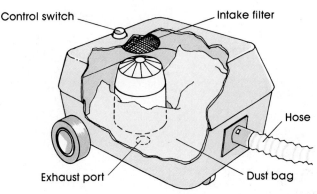

Control switch · Intake filter · Exhaust port · Hose · Dust bag

Upright Vacuum

On upright vacuums, dirt and dust must flow through the inner mechanism to the bag. Small objects such as coins or pins can ruin the fan, or stick in the beater brush, causing the drive belt to break. Be sure to pick up such objects before you vacuum.

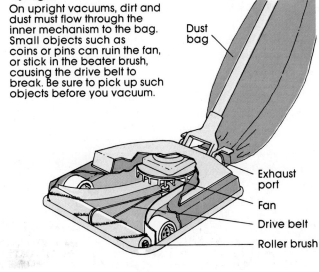

Dust bag · Exhaust port · Fan · Drive belt · Roller brush

PESTS

Black ants

Carpet beetles and larvae

Wherever you live, you are bound to have to deal with household pests. Fortunately, most of them are relatively easy to eradicate. Determine which pests you are dealing with, and find the quickest, most effective way to get rid of them. If you feel threatened by a major invasion and you don't want to handle the situation yourself, call a professional exterminator for help—look under "Pest Control" in the Yellow Pages. Obtain several estimates, and ask about their methods and the chemicals they will be using. You may have to stay out of the house temporarily while it is being treated. If you live in an apartment or rented home, it is often the landlord's responsibility to deal with such problems. Check your lease, and discuss the problem with him. Effective prevention methods include adequate ventilation, cleanliness, caulking and weatherstripping, and moisture control—most pests thrive in a damp environment.

Ants

Ants enter the house to find food, which they then carry to their nests. The nests are usually outside, but may be indoors in protected locations.

To eliminate: Destroy ant trails and nests by spraying them and the surrounding soil with diazinon spray, *or* by treating the anthills with diazinon granules. You can also use ant baits, which the ants take back to their nests. To prevent infestation, store food in sealed containers, and keep kitchens and pantries free of exposed food.

Carpet beetles

The larvae of these beetles damage carpets, furs, clothes, upholstery, and other household products. Some species also feed on stored foods. The beetles fly into homes during the late spring or early summer and may lay their eggs in cracks or crevices, or on clothes, carpets, and other materials. The emerging larvae seek out dark, undisturbed locations in which to feed. They shed their skins a number of times during their development. Most of the larvae hibernate during the winter, and pupate in the spring.

To eliminate: Shake out, brush, and air infested clothes and blankets. To kill remaining larvae, dry clean infested items. Pack clean clothes with paradichlorobenzene crystals in closets or containers. Vacuum or sweep infested rooms, and destroy the sweepings immediately. Kill remaining insects by treating rooms with diazinon *or* a registered spray. Apply according to label directions. Seek professional help to protect carpets and furs.

Clothes moths

These insects chew holes in clothing, blankets, carpets, pillows, upholstery, and other items. Infested articles may be covered with a webbing of silken tubes, cases, and strands. Shiny white caterpillars may be seen crawling on damaged items. These larvae pupate in cocoons attached to the silky web-bing on the infested item, and emerge as adult moths. New infestations occur when moths lay eggs on clothing, carpets, and other articles, and when moth-, larva-, and egg-ridden items are stored with uninfested articles.

To eliminate: Shake out, brush, and air infested clothes and blankets in a sunny location. To kill remaining moths, dry clean infested items. Pack clean clothes with paradichlorobenzene crystals in closets and containers. Vacuum or sweep infested rooms, and destroy the sweepings immediately. Seek professional help to protect carpets and furs.

Cockroaches

Cockroaches infest the kitchen, bathroom, and other areas of the home. In large numbers, they emit a fetid odor. In addition to their annoying presence, cockroaches spread diseases by contaminating food with their infected droppings. These pests proliferate in warm areas where food and water are available—in houses throughout the world. Cockroaches prefer starchy foods, but will feed on any human food scraps, garbage, paper, or fabrics soiled with food. Unless infestations are heavy, or the hiding places are disturbed, cockroaches are rarely seen in exposed locations during the day. These nocturnal insects seek out dark, protected areas in which to live and breed. Usually they congregate in kitchens and bathrooms. They may be found behind or under sinks, refrigerators, and water heaters, within the walls of household appliances, behind baseboards and molding, in wall voids, around pipes, in garbage cans, and in piles of cluttered paper or grocery bags. They may be present in cracks or crevices in cupboards, cabinets, desks, dressers, and closets. They may infest basements, crawl spaces, and sewers. Cockroaches move from one room to another through wall voids or through cracks in walls, floors, and ceilings, and along pipes and conduits. If their living conditions become too crowded, they may migrate. Infestations usually begin when stray insects or egg cases are brought into the home with shipped items, second-hand furniture or appliances, grocery bags, or debris. They may also move into homes from sewers.

To eliminate: Keep the kitchen and other areas of the home free of food scraps. Clean up the kitchen after each meal and store food in tightly sealed metal, glass, or heavy plastic containers or in the refrigerator. Empty household garbage and pet litter regularly. Do not leave garbage and pet food out overnight. Fix leaking faucets and pipes. Clean up water puddles or moist areas around the kitchen, basement, and other infested areas. Plug cracks around baseboards, shelves, cupboards, sinks, and pipes with a filling material such as putty or caulk. Remove food and utensils, then spray with diazinon, resmethrin, or chlorpyrifos in cracks in cupboards, surfaces underneath sinks, along molding, behind appliances, and in other areas where insects are likely to congregate. Allow the spray to dry, then reline the shelves with fresh paper before replacing food and utensils. Bait with a registered bait such as propoxor according to label directions. A registered boric acid dust may also be used. Follow label directions. If infestations are severe or persistent, contact a professional pest-control operator.

Houseflies

These insect pests are common throughout the world. In addition to inflicting their annoying presence, they also can spread a number of serious human diseases and parasites. Flies feed on and lay their eggs in decaying organic materials. The eggs hatch within several days, and even within 12 hours if conditions are ideal. The creamy-white maggots burrow into and feed on the decaying material for several days, pupate, and then emerge as adult flies, which usually live for 15 to 25 days.

To eliminate: To reduce the fly population, maintain sanitary conditions in the home and garden.

Keep garbage covered tightly, and dispose of it regularly. Keep door and window screens in good condition. Kill flies indoors with a registered pesticide such as resmethrin or pyrethrin. Kill flies outdoors with a pesticide containing propoxur, malathion, resmethrin, or diazinon. Apply according to label directions.

Pantry moths and beetles

Beetles and the larvae of moths infest grain products, dried fruits, nuts, and powdered milk. Even when infested packages are removed, the beetles can live on flour and cereals that sift into cracks in the cupboard. They are often brought into the house with packages of food, invading nearby uncontaminated foods that are kept in unsealed, broken, or flimsy containers.

To eliminate: Discard all infested food. Clean out cupboards thoroughly before restocking. If infestation is widespread, remove all food and utensils, and fog the infested area with an insect fogger, or spray shelves and cracks in the pantry with an insecticide. Do not spray countertops or other food areas. Reline shelves with paper and replace food after the spray has dried. If you suspect that food is infested, kill the eggs, larvae, and pupae by deep-freezing food for 4 days or heating it in a shallow pan at 150°F for half an hour. Keep foods in airtight glass, plastic, or metal containers. Keep the pantry clean, and avoid buying broken packages (they are more likely to be infested).

Powderpost beetles

Found in wood flooring, structural timbers, cabinets, furniture, and other items, these insects bore round holes 1/16 to 3/8 inch in size. Wood powder or tiny pellets may be piled around the holes or on the floor below. When the infested item is tapped, additional pellets or wood powder are expelled from the holes. Beetles may be seen crawling around the infested wood, or flying around windows and electric lights in the evening.

Red flour beetle

Powderpost beetle

To eliminate: If the infestation is localized, remove and destroy badly infested timbers. Replace with kiln-dried or insecticide-treated wood. *Or* treat unfinished wood yourself by painting or spraying it with deodorized kerosene. Whenever possible, apply paint, shellac, varnish, paraffin wax, or other wood coatings to unfinished wood around the home to prevent further infestation. Inspect wood piles periodically for signs of powderpost beetle infestation. Store wood away from the structure, or in a cold location. Burn up the supply before beetles emerge in warm weather. If the infestation is widespread, contact a professional pest-control operator to fumigate the building. Individual pieces of furniture may also be fumigated to kill beetle eggs and larvae—many pest-control operators maintain fumigation chambers for portable items. Eggs and larvae in small wooden items may be killed by placing them in the freezer for 4 days.

Silverfish

Black widow spider

Rats and mice

You may see or hear these pests in the attic, garage, basements, wall voids, or other areas of the home. Or you may find signs of infestation, including: droppings; tracks; gnawed doors, baseboards, and cabinets; or loosely constructed nests made of rags, paper, and other scraps. Books, fabrics, furniture, and other objects may be chewed or shredded, and packages of food may be gnawed open and the contents eaten. Rats and mice are notorious for contaminating food with their urine, droppings, and hair, and for spreading parasites and diseases. They are generally active at night.

To eliminate: Control rodents in the home by trapping them. They are more likely to seek bait in traps if their normal source of food is scarce. Remove food from areas where they can get to it easily. Store food in glass or tin containers with screw-on or otherwise tightly sealed lids. Place traps where droppings, gnawings, and damage indicate their presence—behind refrigerators and other protective objects, in dark corners, along baseboards, and in cupboards. Bait mouse traps with pieces of bacon, nutmeats, raisins, or peanut butter. Bait rat traps with pieces of beef, bacon, fish, nutmeats, or carrots. Tie the bait to the trigger so the animal won't be able to remove the bait without springing the trap. Attach wire to rat traps so the traps cannot be dragged away. Check the traps daily to dispose of trapped rats and mice. Wear gloves when handling them, or pick them up with tongs to avoid being bitten by their parasites. You also can use poisoned baits. If you are unable to eliminate all the pests, contact a professional pest-control operator. To prevent rats and mice from returning, seal holes or cracks larger than ¼ inch leading into the building from outside. For details on rodent-proofing your home, contact your local Cooperative Extension Office.

Silverfish and firebrats

These insects chew and stain paper and fabric products, especially those made with glue, paste, or other starchy materials. Flattened, slender, wingless insects; excrement; and silver or gray scales may fall out when infested products are moved. Silverfish prefer damp, cool to warm (70° to 80°F) locations such as basements and wall voids. Firebrats prefer damp, hot (90° to 105°F) locations such as hot-water pipes and areas near the oven or furnace. These pests are active at night, and they hide during the day. They feed on a wide range of foods, especially products high in starches, including human food, paper, paste, and linen and other fabrics. Silverfish damage books by feeding on the bindings. These pests crawl throughout the house along pipes and through holes or crevices in the walls or floor.

To eliminate: Spray with chlorpyrifos, diazinon, or other registered spray according to label directions. Where practical, seal all cracks and crevices in the infested areas. Store valued papers and clothes in tightly sealed plastic bags.

Spiders

There are two common poisonous spiders in the United States: black widow spiders and brown recluse spiders. Black widow spiders are found throughout the country. Outdoors, they live under rocks or clods of dirt, or in wood and rubbish piles. Indoors, they are found in garages, attics, cellars, and other dark, secluded places—under boards or cluttered debris, in old clothing, or in crevices. Their webs are coarse and irregular, about 1 foot wide. Brown recluse spiders are found in the Midwest and Southeast—outdoors under rocks, and indoors in old boxes, among papers and old clothes, behind baseboards, underneath tables and chairs, and in other secluded places. Their webs are grayish, irregular, and sticky. Either spider will bite if touched or trapped. The brown recluse is very shy, moving away quickly when disturbed; the black widow is more likely to be aggressive, especially when guarding her nest. The venom of the black widow may cause serious illness and possibly death to young or old people. The brown recluse venom causes a severe sore that is extremely slow to heal, and may require surgery. Put ice on spider bites, and call a doctor immediately.

To eliminate: Kill spiders by fogging with a registered pesticide or spraying webs and infested areas with chlorpyrifos, diazinon, resmethrin, or propoxur. Remove loose wood, trash, and clutter from areas where spiders might hide. Wear protective clothing and gloves when cleaning up infested areas. Vacuum infested areas to remove egg sacs, and destroy the contents of the vacuum-cleaner bag.

Subterranean termites

You may see these insects or their discarded wings around buildings after a rain on warm, sunny spring or fall days. Subterranean termites cause more structural damage to buildings than does any other type of insect. Look in basements and crawlspaces for earthen tubes extending from the soil up along the foundation and any other termite-proof surface to the wooden members above. Dark or blistered areas may develop in the flooring. When buildings are erected over established termite colonies, serious damage may occur within as little as a year. They hollow out the inside of boards, leaving only an outer shell. Damage is most severe when they infest main supporting wooden beams and girders.

To eliminate: Termite infestations can be treated most effectively only after a thorough and accurate diagnosis of the damage has been made. This usually very difficult procedure requires the aid of a professional termite operator or pest-control operator. Once the operator has located the termite colony and revealed the damage, he or she places a physical or chemical barrier between the soil and the building to prevent the termites from reaching the building. If infestations are small and localized, you may control them by applying chlordane or another registered pesticide to the soil, according to label directions. Discourage additional infestations by keeping the area under and around the house free of wood debris above and below the ground. Termites prefer moist soil. If the soil around the foundation remains moist due to faulty plumbing or improper grade, repair the plumbing and alter the grade.

Round-headed borers

You may see these beetles around the house, or hear a rasping or ticking sound behind wallcoverings, plaster, linoleum, and wood. Look for sawdustlike borings around irregular holes; or, if the borers are tunneling close to the surface, blisters. There are two species that do damage in a house. Most round-head borers do not cause structural damage—the holes they make in wood or covered wood surfaces are of cosmetic concern only. They will emerge from the holes up to a year after new construction and will not reenter.

To eliminate: Seal or fill emergence holes. Old-house borers do not emerge from timbers until from three to five years after the building has been constructed. They continue to reinfest and cause damage to wood, and may cause serious structural damage. Buildings with old-house borers must be fumigated by a professional pest-control operator. To prevent future infestations, purchase pressure-treated wood when building new structures.

Pesticides

By law, pesticide labels must carry important information and precautions. Read the directions carefully. Dilute, apply, and dispose of pesticides exactly as recommended. Following these directions also will give you the best results. Read the precautions carefully. The most toxic chemicals are marked with a skull and crossbones and the words "Danger—Poison." The word "Warning" on the label means that the product is moderately toxic and that you should use recommended precautions. The word "Caution," when it appears by itself, means that the chemical is mildly toxic. "Caution. Keep out of reach of children" appears on *all* pesticide labels. Store and use pesticides well away from children and pets. Some insecticides may stain or damage fibers, leather, and plastics, so read the entire label before using. The label usually indicates what to do in case someone is inadvertently exposed to the chemical. If accidental ingestion occurs, contact a physician immediately. Ortho products list an emergency telephone number in case of accident. The label also has information on storing and disposing of leftover pesticide. Some products are flammable, some lose their effectiveness in time, and some must be disposed of in special ways. The label indicates the manufacturer, specific ingredients, and

Subterranean termites

whether the product is restricted to official use (it is illegal for non-professionals to use highly restricted chemicals).

Common insecticides

Chlorpyrifos: Widely used indoor and outdoor insecticide on lawns. Effective on fleas and ticks and common nuisance pests. Residual life of about 6 to 8 weeks outdoors. Moderately toxic.

Diazinon: An effective insecticide for both indoor and outdoor use. Dilute and apply according to label instructions. Sometimes combined with other chemicals. Moderately toxic.

Lindane: Not for indoor use. Used to control powderpost beetles and outdoor pests. Moderately toxic.

Malathion: A very effective outdoor pesticide with a relatively low toxicity. Strong smell.

Propoxur: Effective in controlling indoor and outdoor pests. Has a long residual life inside (45 days). Moderately toxic.

Pyrethrin: To control flying insects. Usually in aerosol form. Made from chrysanthemums. Its effects last only a few hours. Probably the safest, least toxic insecticide available (although it may cause allergy problems).

Resmethrin: Mostly used indoors on nuisance pests. Can be used to control fleas on dogs and cats. Short residual life. Slightly toxic.

Sevin: A broad-spectrum pesticide used to control garden pests and fleas and ticks on animals. Slightly toxic.

The most effective ways to prevent odors are cleanliness, adequate ventilation, and quick action so that a pervasive odor cannot penetrate into walls and furnishings. Exhaust fans in bathrooms and kitchens—as well as air purifiers, open windows, and regular airing of clothes, rooms, and furnishings—all help eliminate offensive odors. Common odors—and what to do about them—are listed below.

Air conditioners: Unplug the conditioner and wipe with a solution of ½ gal water and a few tbsp chlorine bleach. Replace the filter if it has mold or mildew on it. If the unit contains water, add a few drops of alcohol *or* bottled lemon juice to freshen it.

Ashtrays: Wipe with a paper towel dampened with alcohol to clean and remove stale tobacco odor.

Baby bottles: Place a few tsp baking soda into the bottle, fill with hot water, and let sit for several hours. Wash in hot, soapy water using a bottle brush. Rinse.

Bathrooms: Use a commercial room deodorizer. If the room is musty, wipe with a mild chlorine-bleach solution, *or* use a commercial mildew remover.

Cigarette and cigar smoke: Open bowls of vinegar and lighted candles will absorb smoke during a party. When guests leave, open the windows, dampen a towel with equal parts vinegar and water, and swish it through the air. Air smoke-filled clothing outdoors, *or* in the clothes dryer with a fabric softener sheet, *or* with a fan. Place open jars or cans of vinegar, charcoal, *or* baking soda in closets; use a wick-type room deodorizer *or* air-freshening spray; *or* boil whole cloves or cardamom seeds in water.

Drawers: Line clothes drawers with scented drawer paper. You can also paint the underside of the drawers with cedar oil, *or* use sachets of lavender or potpourri; *or* add an unwrapped soap bar.

Fireplaces: Noxious smells from your fire generally mean you are inadvertently burning plastic, rubber, or paint. Clean out the ashes when they are cool, and scrape up any melted material. Throw a handful of citrus peel on the next fire, *or* burn commercial fire incense *or* aromatic woods.

Furnaces: If you smell odors when you turn on your furnace, check the registers and ducts, and vacuum out any dust or debris.

Furniture: If your furniture smells musty, treat first for mildew by wiping the undersides with a mild chlorine-bleach solution. Brush a scented lacquer or cedar oil on the undersides of tables and chairs to make them smell fresh. Upholstered furniture that smells musty or bad should be cleaned professionally.

Garbage cans: Clean regularly with hot water and a disinfectant cleaner. Rinse with the hose, and spray with ammonia to repel animals and insects.

Garbage disposals: Eliminate odors by grinding up orange or lemon peels with hot running water.

Gas: If you smell natural gas and can't identify the source quickly, leave the house leaving a window or door open, and call the fire department immediately. A tiny spark or pilot light can ignite a gas leak and cause a fire.

Gasoline: Add a little chlorine bleach to the laundry to

Use potpourris, scented soaps and candles, spices, and pomander balls to add pleasant scents to your rooms.

eliminate gasoline odor on clothing. To remove the smell from your hands, rub with with lemon juice *or* vinegar.

Humidifiers: To keep humidifiers smelling fresh, add bottled lemon juice *or* alcohol to the water.

Kerosene: When using kerosene, place an open bowl of vinegar in the room, and rinse your hands in vinegar to neutralize the smell. When washing clothes that smell of kerosene, add 1 c vinegar to the final rinse.

Kitchen: Most food odors can be eliminated by boiling a pan of white vinegar on top of the stove, *or* by turning on the exhaust fan. You need a fairly powerful exhaust fan that vents to the outside so that it will pull enough air out of the room to get rid of odors. Freshen your kitchen by boiling a few whole cloves *or* cardamom seeds in a pan of water.

Linen closets: Place unwrapped scented soaps or sachets among your linens, *or* line the shelves with scented paper.

Mildew and mold: Mold and mildew can be eliminated only if the fungus itself is controlled. Wipe hard surfaces with a mild chlorine-bleach solution *or* a commercial mildew spray. Wipe or spray mattresses and box springs with a disinfectant spray. If the bed is already badly mildewed, it will have to be cleaned professionally or replaced. Empty out musty closets and wipe the insides with a mild bleach solution. Allow to dry, and wipe the walls and floor with cedar oil. An open can of charcoal or silicone crystals will help you keep down fungus-encouraging moisture. Dry out the can in a warm oven for 15 minutes every few months. Wash or dry clean affected clothing. Air musty shoes outside on a sunny day, or in front of a fan. Air the house regularly, and control moisture with adequate heating and ventilation and vapor barriers on the warm side of walls and floors.

Moth crystals: A good airing with open doors and windows or a fan will help dissipate the smell of the crystals within a few days. Hang clothes outside. To eliminate the smell quickly, wipe closets and luggage with equal parts alcohol *or* vinegar, and water.

New paint: To keep away the odor of new paint, open the windows and doors, and use fans while you work. Adding a few drops of vanilla extract to the paint will make the smell more pleasant. A large peeled onion in a pan of cold water close to where you're working will help absorb the smell.

Onion and garlic: To eliminate the smell from your hands, rub them with vinegar *or* lemon juice.

Perspiration: To get rid of perspiration odors on washable clothes, pre-soak with an enzyme product *or* rinse with vinegar. Turn non-washable garments inside out and hang outside for a few hours, *or* in the bathroom, where the steam will help dissipate the smell. A wick-type air freshener *or* can of charcoal in the closet will also help.

Plastic food containers: To deodorize, freeze containers for several hours or run them through the dishwasher.

Radiators: To impart a pleasant odor to the room, sprinkle the radiator with a few drops oil of wintergreen *or* vanilla, *or* place a saucer of whole cloves *or* cardamom seeds underneath it.

Refrigerator-freezer: Keep strong-smelling foods wrapped, and periodically clean out old food. Wipe appliance clean with a solution of baking soda and water, *or* vinegar. To absorb odors, place an open box of baking soda *or* charcoal (use the kind made for fish aquariums or house plants) *or* an open jar of vinegar *or* dried coffee grounds in the refrigerator. You can also saturate cotton balls with oil of wintergreen *or* vanilla extract and place them in a saucer at the back of the refrigerator.

Sickrooms: Keep open bowls of vinegar in inconspicuous corners. When the sick person is out of the room, spray the air lightly with a disinfectant spray, and then ventilate the room.

Sinks: To eliminate odors and keep drains unclogged, mix ½ c baking soda and ½ c vinegar with a kettle of boiling water, and pour the solution down the drain.

Thermos bottles: Fill the thermos with a solution of baking soda and hot water and let sit for a couple of hours before washing.

Skunk: There is nothing you can do to get rid of the odor of skunk in the air except mask it and wait until it dissipates. If you or your dog are sprayed by a skunk, try rubbing dog, clothes, and yourself with tomato juice. Then wash in hot, soapy water. A product commercially available in pet stores will help remove the odor.

Trash compactor: Wrap foods before putting them in the compactor. Sprinkle garbage with baking soda *or* vinegar. Do not put fish, bones, or strong cheeses in the machine—dispose in outdoor garbage can instead. Periodically clean the ram that pushes the garbage down into the compactor according to your owner's manual. Use hot, soapy water and ammonia *or* vinegar.

Vacuum cleaner: Empty or replace cleaner bags often. To impart a fresh scent to the room as you vacuum, place several cotton balls saturated with oil of wintergreen *or* vinegar on the floor and vacuum them up.

Vases: To keep water fresh, add charcoal chips (available from nurseries) to the water.

Pets

Most difficulties with pets are easy to remedy. This section deals with solutions to the most common household problems associated with pets.

□ **To keep pets out of your garbage cans:** Sprinkle both the garbage and the can with full-strength ammonia *or* a commercial spray designed to repel animals. To keep cans from being overturned, place them inside old tires *or* on a platform with 2 by 4s nailed around it.

□ **To discourage pets from sitting on or scratching furniture:** Place wrapped packages of camphor (available from a pharmacy) under cushions—most animals are repelled by the smell.

□ **To protect your garden from pets:** Spray around the perimeter of cultivated beds with a commercial animal repellent.

□ **To prevent and eliminate fleas in the house:** The problem with fleas is not only their itchy bites—they also can carry diseases (such as bubonic plague) and some parasitic worms (such as tape worm). Keep your pets and their resting places free of fleas, with flea collars, powders, and baths. Sprinkle powdered brewer's yeast onto your pet's food—most animals like the taste of it, and the B vitamins make the pet unpalatable to fleas. The ideal environment for a flea is a warm, damp area. The closer to ideal it is, the sooner the reproductive cycle begins and ends—at best (or worst) two weeks. Eggs can lay dormant for more than a year until the right temperature and humidity allow them to hatch. After hatching, fleas respond to anything that moves, and to body warmth—you and your pets. You may have fleas even if you have no pets: Neighboring pets can infest your lawn, fleas may be brought in on your clothing, or they may show up after you have entertained a friend's pet. Treat an infested lawn with a Sevin garden dust (available at nursery and hardware stores) at the same time that you treat your pet and the inside of your house. Sevin can also be used as a flea powder—follow label instructions carefully. Get rid of fleas indoors with an indoor insect fogger or spray. Follow package directions exactly. You may have to repeat the process to ensure that all the eggs, larvae, and adults are dead. Vacuum carpets, upholstered furniture, and pet beds daily until pests are gone. Empty the cleaner bag into a plastic bag each time you vacuum, or the fleas may escape.

□ **To clean up pet accidents:** Pet accident odors are difficult to eradicate—especially if the accidents have happened more than once in the same place. Scrape up solids, and blot liquids. Sponge with warm, soapy water. Sprinkle dry baking soda or a commercial carpet-odor powder on the area and leave on for several hours, then vacuum up. If your carpets are made of synthetic fibers, you can apply a paste of enzyme product and water. Leave it on for half an hour, then sponge up, rinse, and blot dry. A product that is commercially available at pet stores is very effective in removing pet odors. Use the same methods on hard floor surfaces. Be certain to clean the vacuum thoroughly to prevent the enzyme product or carpet deodorizers from corroding the metal parts of the machine.

YOUR HOME'S SYSTEMS & EXTERIOR

A periodic check of all your
home's systems and exterior is
a critical aspect of home care.
This chapter helps you recognize
and deal with potential problems
before they develop into expensive,
major repairs.

When you approach a house, you may get a first impression about the people who live inside, particularly from the level of attention given both to the style of the house and to the landscape. A well-swept path and sparkling-clean windows can make you feel welcome before you knock on the door. Even unseen parts of a house, such as the heating, cooling, electrical, and plumbing systems, affect your overall sense of a home's condition. Properly maintained internal systems—all the lights and heating ducts working, no plumbing leaks, sound wiring—give the sense that things "work" in this house, that daily activities can proceed unhampered by annoying problems. Upkeep involves caring for your home's structure, exterior, and systems as much as it does cleaning the interior. The basic difference is that these maintenance tasks are done sporadically rather than routinely. This chapter tells you how to conduct periodic maintenance checks so you can prevent expensive major repairs.

If you take care of potential problems early, they won't become time-consuming, expensive repairs. The longer you neglect a hole in your blacktop driveway, the larger and harder to fix it will become. If you don't remove weeds before they go to seed in the fall, they will be harder to remove later on. It's also important to deal with maintenance tasks at appropriate times: Have your air conditioner checked and serviced before summer, your chimney cleaned before winter, and your gutters cleaned out before the rainy season.

Just as professionals can help you maintain your home's interior, so they can help with your home's exterior, systems, and landscape. To find professional exterior cleaners, look in the Yellow Pages under "Janitorial Maintenance." To find an electrician, a plumber, or a heating, cooling, or pest-control professional, look under those specific heads. For help with your garden, look under "Landscape Maintenance," or in the newspaper under "Jobs Wanted." Make sure the professionals you hire

are bonded or insured. They should be willing to guarantee their work, and before they proceed with any work you should both agree about what they will do, what their charge will be, and when they will start and finish the job.

Each section in this chapter describes the parts of your house you should check periodically for potential problems, and tells you what to do if you find any suspicious symptoms. Moisture, for example, is one of the biggest household problems. Because moisture often starts in your foundation, basement, or crawlspace, this chapter's first section tells you how to determine the source of the moisture, and how to repair and prevent moisture damage.

The section on roofs, chimneys, and attics leads you through a maintenance check for such things as loose shingles or gutters, chimney cracks, and roof leaks.

"Exterior Walls and Windows" contains information on how to clean and repair various siding materials, including brick, and how to clean windows like professional window washers.

Because the garage is a very common source of household fires, the garage section on pages 80–81 focuses on a check for safety hazards. It tells you how to examine the structure for such problems as dry rot and insects.

The information on pages 82–88 will help you become familiar with your home's electrical, plumbing, heating, and cooling systems. This familiarity will help you know when to call in a professional to repair these systems and how to locate power sources and water shut-off valves throughout your house in case of emergency. You'll also learn how to check your outlets for grounding and your wood stove for fire safety.

The final section tells how to make minor repairs on decks, walkways, patios, and driveways. Schedules for maintaining landscapes and year-round swimming pools outline when to do seasonal tasks.

As this chapter—and the entire book—reveals, home care and upkeep are easier and far less costly when you attend to your home on an ongoing basis and keep ahead of potential problems.

Caring for your home's exterior on a routine,
semi-annual basis helps you keep it in the best possible
condition.

BASEMENTS & CRAWLSPACES

Foundations

A sound foundation will prevent the moisture and insect problems that can wreak havoc in your house. Cracks in the foundation walls are not unusual or necessarily serious while a house is still settling, but to prevent moisture problems in the interim, patch them as they occur. Cracks may continue to appear until the settling process has slowed down. Because settling is caused by unequal shifts in the soil, which themselves are caused by moisture, make certain you have good drainage all around the house. Check for outdoor plumbing leaks, and low spots where water can collect and oversaturate the soil in one spot. If you have a serious water problem, keep plants at least 18 inches away from the foundation. Periodically check your foundation for:

1. Cracks in the foundation walls, and in all junctures between the walls and patios, walks, and driveways: Fill with patching cement.

2. Gaps around doors, windows, vents, and any other openings: Seal with silicone caulking, *or* weatherstripping.

3. Signs of structural damage from settling: These include large cracks or bowing in the foundation walls, sloping floors inside, and doors or windows that stick or no longer fit their frames. If you find such symptoms, see Ortho's book, *Basic Home Repairs*, or contact a professional.

4. Signs of insects: See Pests, pages 66–69.

Crawlspaces

With a flashlight, crawl under your house and look around, *or* look through vents or openings around the foundation. Check:

1. Posts or piers and support framing: Check wood for signs of mold, rot, or termites. See the following material on water and termites for symptoms. Replace damaged wood.

2. Standing water: If you see water and there is no sump pump, consider installing one to drain water away from structural supports.

3. Vapor barriers on bare ground: If your first floor is cold and damp in the winter, and there are no vapor barriers on the bare ground of your crawlspace, you can eliminate the problem: Measure the area, adding an extra 5 inches around the edges for lap. Lay 2-mil-thick polyethylene sheeting on the ground. Staple or nail to the crawlspace walls and weight down with bricks.

4. Subfloor insulation: Check that the vapor barrier is on the floor side, that it is not visible from the crawlspace, and that it is not loose or missing sections.

5. Water pipes: Repair leaky pipes. In cold-weather areas, insulate pipes on exterior walls to prevent freezing. See Ortho's book, *Energy-Saving Projects for the Home.*

6. Cold-air return ducts: Ducts should be well off the ground and securely connected; otherwise they will send frigid, musty air into your rooms. They can also develop holes from rust. Insulate them to prevent these problems.

7. Outside vents and doors: Cover with screening to keep animals from getting under the house.

Checking for Moisture Problems

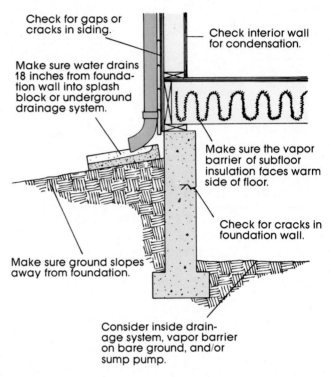

Check for gaps or cracks in siding.

Check interior wall for condensation.

Make sure water drains 18 inches from foundation wall into splash block or underground drainage system.

Make sure the vapor barrier of subfloor insulation faces warm side of floor.

Make sure ground slopes away from foundation.

Check for cracks in foundation wall.

Consider inside drainage system, vapor barrier on bare ground, and/or sump pump.

Basements

Musty odors, mildew, damp walls, puddles on the floor, or even flooding will tell you that you have a moisture problem. The following sections on condensation, seepage, and leaks will help you diagnose, correct, and prevent these problems. In addition, check the basement for:

1. Flammable materials and clutter: Store flammable materials away from heat sources and in metal containers. Get rid of the clutter. Make certain that wood paneling is not too near heating sources.

2. Support beams: Look for sags or gaps between beams and girders. Contact a professional for advice.

3. Exterior windows, doors, vents, and pipes: Make certain that these (particularly bulkhead doors) are well sealed with caulking and weatherstripping.

4. Insulation: The vapor barriers for the basement walls should face the room.

Special problems

The number one problem with basements, foundations, and crawlspaces is excess moisture in the form of condensation, seepage, or leaks. Aside from creating discomfort, moisture can also cause structural damage from wet rot and dry rot, and can encourage insects. Before buying or even renting a house, ask the former occupants or neighbors whether they have had any serious moisture problems and whether the area is subject to flooding.

Condensation

If your basement is damp or musty only during hot weather, if your cold-water pipes "sweat" on hot days, or if puddles appear on the floor in the summer, chances are the problem is condensation—cool surfaces collecting moisture from the warm air. To solve:

1. Wrap the water pipes with insulation.
2. Improve the cross-ventilation in the basement by opening the doors and windows more often, and by using a fan to keep the air moving through the room. Install more vents in the walls.
3. Install a dehumidifier and/or permanent fan.

Seepage and leaks

If you have mildew in the basement or crawlspace, if the house is damp periodically throughout the year, or if water trickles down the walls and puddles on the floor, the problem may be seepage. Because the symptoms for condensation and seepage are similar, use this test to find out which problem you have: Tape a strip of foil tightly to both the wall and the floor. Leave it on for a few days, then check it. If it's wet on the wall side, you have a seepage problem; if it's wet on the room side, it's condensation. If the foil is wet on both sides, it's both.

Most causes of seepage and leaks are external—too much water in the soil near the foundation walls. The symptoms described above, or peeling paint, water stains, efflorescence (white deposits) on walls or floors, rusty nails, pipes or ducts mean you have a long-standing problem. Correct it as soon as possible. The most common causes and some solutions are listed below.

1. Plumbing, heating, and cooling systems: Check for leaks in exposed hoses and pipes, blocked air ducts, overflowing water containers, broken underground pipes, overflowing sewer, malfunctioning sump pump, or cracked pipes behind the walls.
2. Walls and floors: Check for cracks between wall and floor, or in the mortar between cinder blocks and bricks. Patch any cracks you find with patching compound. If the crack is wet, you can repair it with a fast-setting hydraulic cement, available at hardware stores. Patching cracks will not resolve the problem if external water pressure and saturation are serious.
3. Gutters and downspouts: Keep gutters clear of debris. Downspouts should deposit water at least 18 inches away from foundation walls, or connect to an underground drainage system. Make certain the system is not blocked at any point. If you have a drywell, make certain it is not full and backing up.
4. Garden edgings: Bricks, metal strips, or rocks used to edge the garden should not form a dam, trapping water near the foundation. Remove them if necessary.
5. Slope of ground: The ground should slope away from the house—1 inch every 6 feet. If it is level or slopes toward the house, add soil to create the proper slope—directing water away from the foundation. If a patio, driveway, or walkway slopes toward the house, consider installing curbs to keep the water flowing past, not toward, the house.

6. Foundation: Check the foundation for waterproofing. Pick a spot near your inside moisture problem, and dig down into the soil. Look for black asphaltic mastic applied to the wall. If you don't see any, your walls may not be waterproofed. Although exterior waterproofing is far superior to interior waterproofing, you can try painting the inside walls with a special waterproofing paint. Consult a dealer at your local hardware store or home improvement center.
7. Contact a professional: If all the above steps fail, you may need to install a sump pump in your crawlspace, a drainage system around the interior perimeter of your basement, or to improve your drainage system outside. These are more extensive and expensive alternatives. But if water is a big problem, they may be necessary.

Dry rot

Dry rot is a fungus spread by spores. It looks reddish and puffy and may smell musty. Look for it under suspended ground floors. To test for dry rot, poke suspicious timbers with an ice pick—dry rot works from the inside out. If your wood has dry rot, the damaged sections will have to be replaced with wood that has been treated to resist fungi. Prevent dry rot by keeping the area as dry and airy as possible.

Insects

The most common insect pests are termites and wood-boring beetles. Check for: mud tunnels running up your foundation walls, entrance and exit holes, and piles of fine sawdust. Check wood piles and fences as well. Remove all loose wood on the ground close to the house and in crawlspaces, and store wood well away from the house. Watch for swarming termites and their discarded wings near the house on warm, sunny spring or fall days. If you suspect a major infestation, call a pest-control company for an inspection. For more complete information on how to recognize and eliminate insect damage, see Pests, pages 66–69.

Mildew

Mildew is a fungus caused by excess moisture. It cannot grow in a dry environment. Determine the source of the moisture, and eliminate it if possible. In the interim, exhaust the excess with a dehumidifier or exhaust fan, and regularly air the affected rooms. To kill mildew, wipe it with a solution of chlorine bleach and water, or by spraying it with a commercial mildew remover. Trim back the bushes and trees that are blocking air and sunlight from the mildewed area. Never paint over mildew—it will continue to grow under the paint.

Wet rot

Wet-rot fungus thrives on wood (although the wood generally has to be kept very wet) and works from the outside in. The wood looks and feels spongy, and deteriorates rapidly. Painted wood that shows signs of chipped paint may be infested. Replace infested wood with wood that has been treated to resist fungi. Prevent wet rot by eliminating the source of the water.

ROOFS, ATTICS & CHIMNEYS

Roofs

Check the roof for sources of leaks and for structural problems. Look at the roof through binoculars from the ground, or on a ladder placed securely against the side of the house. See Ortho's book, *Basic Home Repairs,* for guidelines on using ladders safely. If you do get onto the roof, use caution: don't go up there on a wet or windy day, or if the roof is not completely dry; and do wear soft-soled, non-slip shoes. If your roof is very steep, let a professional do any necessary repairs. The south side is particularly vulnerable to sun damage, so start there. Check as follows:

1. Roofing materials: The life of roofing materials varies considerably, depending on the severity of the weather. In general, asphalt, and tar and gravel will last 20 to 25 years, wood 35 to 40 years, and slate and ceramic tile 35 to 90 years.

☐ *Shingles.* Look for any that have blown away, have worked loose, or are split or curling. Asphalt shingles are generally coated with a coarse sand. When this wears off (you will see black areas), they may be worn out.

☐ *Ceramic tile.* Look for cracked or missing tiles.

☐ *Metal.* Look for badly pitted or rusting metal.

☐ *Flat tar and gravel.* Look for bubbles and bare spots. If you see any of these problems, make immediate repairs because the damaged areas will eventually leak. See Ortho's book, *Basic Home Repairs,* for small jobs; call a professional for the big ones.

2. Low points: Look for areas where water and leaves have collected—they may be eroding your roofing materials. Keep these areas free of debris when you clean out your gutters in the fall and spring.

3. Ridges and pitch: Check the ridges and pitch (slope) of the roof—they should look regular and even. If they aren't, check the ridge beam and rafters in the attic. An uneven roof indicates structural damage that may be serious; consult a professional.

4. Plumbing vents: Plumbing vents should be visible on the roof. If you don't see them, check the attic—vents that terminate inside the attic violate the plumbing code in most states. Also, vents should not terminate near windows or have other equipment, such as antenna wires, attached to them.

5. Solar equipment: If you have roof-mounted solar equipment, make certain it is fastened securely to the roof. See Ortho's book, *Energy-Saving Projects for the Home,* for more details on solar equipment.

6. Trees: Check nearby trees for dead branches that could fall on the roof. Have these branches removed.

7. Ice dams: Ice dams are symptoms of excessive heat loss through the roof. As the snow melts, it collects in the eaves and gutters, refreezes, and backs up under the roof covering, lifting it and causing leaks. Reduce the amount of heat that escapes by improving the insulation and ventilation in the attic (see Attics, on this page).

Chimneys

Use this section to check the outside of your chimney. To check the inside and the fireplace itself, see Fireplaces, page 88. To repair or install chimney caps, spark arres-ters, raincaps, gutters, and downspouts, see Ortho's book, *Basic Home Repairs.*

1. Outside stack: Check the outside chimney stack for crumbling, cracked, loose, or missing stones, bricks, or mortar. Sparks can escape through cracks to the wood frame of your house, creating a serious fire hazard. Repair them before lighting another fire. Check for gaps between the house and the exterior chimney, and repair with mortar. Make certain the chimney is not leaning. If it is, seek professional advice—a leaning chimney is a serious fire hazard.

2. Chimney cap: Look for cracked, crumbling, or missing sections of the concrete cap. Repair small cracks with exterior caulk or asphalt cement; repair crumbling sections with pre-mixed mortar cement.

3. Spark arrester: Install a wire spark arrester to keep sparks and embers off the roof, and to keep small creatures out of the chimney.

4. Raincap: If you have problems with smoky fires, a raincap will deflect the down draft as well as both rain and snow.

Gutters and downspouts

While you are looking at the roof, check the gutters and downspouts. They are either built in as part of the roof structure and eaves, or mounted to the exterior with metal or plastic clips. In snowbelt areas, they should lie behind the roof's slope so they won't catch the snow that slides off the roof, possibly causing ice dams.

1. Debris: Check for debris and sediment in the late fall and early spring. Remove it with any hand tool, and then flush with a hose. If you don't have leaf traps, consider installing them—clogged gutters cause water to back up and splash over the sides. This erodes the soil below, which can leak into your foundation or basement and possibly damage the siding on the house.

2. Gutter hangers and downspout clips: Reseat and attach loose hangers and clips to the roof and sides of the house. Caulk all joints.

3. Metal gutters and downspouts: Peeling paint will cause rust and leaks later on. Brush off loose paint with a metal brush, and touch up with a paint made especially for metal. Before painting new galvanized metal, wipe it with turpentine or paint thinner to remove the oily coating.

4. Wooden gutters and downspouts: Check for dry rot, and replace affected sections.

5. Downspout extensions: Channel water away from the house with plastic extensions, concrete splash blocks, or drain pipes at the ends of downspouts. Water that pours directly from the downspout onto the ground can erode the soil and seep into the foundation or basement.

Attics

Check your attic for roof leaks, adequate ventilation, and structural soundness. In an unfinished attic, wear a dust mask and take a flashlight. Walk only on the joists—the ceiling below will not support your weight.

1. Insulation: Blown or loose insulation between the floor joists should be distributed evenly. If it has shifted into the

Checking the Roof

Once a year you should check the roof of your house (and garage) to spot potential problems before they become serious (see text). If you use a ladder for your inspection, observe some simple precautions: **1.** Examine the ladder first for cracks and loose rungs. **2.** If you are using a wooden ladder on concrete, nail pieces of rubber onto the bottom of the side rails. **3.** Place the feet away from the house by a distance equal to one-fourth the height of the ladder. **4.** Grip the rails, not the rungs, and keep both hips between the rails at all times.

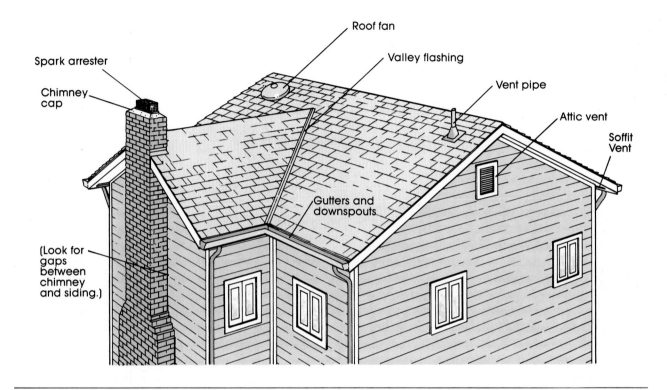

corners, rake it evenly and staple wire screening or kraft paper on top. Be certain to wear a dust mask. Dry out wet insulation with a fan, and open windows to improve ventilation. Make sure that vapor barriers face the floor. If there are two layers of insulation, both with vapor barriers, slit the top barrier so that moisture can ventilate. Tap insulated walls. If they sound hollow at the top, it means the insulation has settled and needs to be replaced or restapled.

2. Leaks: Signs of a leaky roof include dark streaks on the ceiling, wet insulation, and rusty nail heads. Switch off the light and look for daylight through gaps and holes. Push a wire through to the roof to mark for future repairs.

3. Openings: To prevent flames from spreading upward in case of fire, block openings where chimneys, heater ducts, and kitchen or bathroom exhausts come up through the floor. Use a non-flammable material, such as sheet metal. Check that exhaust duct joints are secure. If necessary, push them back together.

4. Plumbing vents: Open plumbing vents should extend through the roof. Vents that terminate inside the attic violate the plumbing codes in most states.

5. Ventilation: Dry rot, damp insulation, or delamination of the plywood on attic walls and ceilings are signs of inadequate ventilation. If your house is too hot in summer or too cold in winter (in spite of good heating and cooling systems and plenty of insulation, or if the attic is damp), improve your ventilation by adding vents or fans. To check for dry rot, poke the joists with an ice pick—dry rot works from the inside out, looks reddish and puffy, and smells musty. If three or more joists are rotted, they could collapse—consult a professional. To improve your ventilation:

□ When the room is being used, open the windows and run a portable house-fan to ventilate the moisture.

□ Install gable vents and/or a gable-mounted fan in the gables; a turbine, cupola, or roof vent on the roof; or a whole-house fan or vent between the floor joists. See Ortho's book, *Energy-Saving Projects for the Home*, for complete instructions on installing all of these.

□ Install additional soffit vents in the eaves, or unblock existing ones.

□ When adding a second story, plan a ventilation tower or cupola vent.

6. Vermin: Check for signs of rats, mice, or squirrels—droppings or nests—in your insulation or stored materials. To eliminate rats and mice, see Pests, pages 66–69.

7. Wiring or electrical fixtures: Look carefully at any exposed wiring or fixtures. If any of it looks makeshift or if there are dangling wires, consult a qualified electrician. For more information on wiring, see Electrical Systems, pages 82–83.

Walls

House siding protects inner walls from damage and should be repaired promptly. Moisture can rot out part of the wall from the inside even before external signs of damage appear. One indication that there may be a problem is paint peeling off the walls in an inside room. Check your siding as indicated below.

Aluminum

Unpainted spots are serious in humid areas; aluminum won't rust, but it will eventually corrode, and should be touched up.

1. Gaps: Caulk any gaps in joints with commercial caulking made especially for aluminum siding.

2. Grounding wire: Aluminum conducts electricity, and should be grounded for safety. Look for a grounding wire running from the siding to a plumbing pipe or a rod in the ground. If you don't see one, call your local building inspector to ask whether it's required in your area, and where you might find it.

3. Torn or loose sections: Replace or renail the siding as described in Ortho's book, *Basic Home Repairs*.

Asbestos shingle

Any damage will probably be near the foundation, where excess moisture often causes the shingles to crack and break off.

1. Brittle, cracked, or broken sections: Replace damaged sections. Repair smaller cracks with asbestos caulking.

2. Loose or rusty nails: Hammer in the loose nails and replace rusty ones with non-rusting types—rusty nails will streak the siding. Check for the source of excess moisture; it may be pushing nails out and causing them to rust.

Brick, concrete, or concrete block

Ortho's book, *Basic Home Repairs*, discusses major repairs on these materials.

1. Cracks: Long, vertical cracks may indicate that the house is still settling. To find out, mark both sides of the crack with black waterproof marker. Measure and record the width of the crack. Check after several months. If the measurement has changed by even $1/16$ inch, or if the marker lines no longer coincide, the house is still settling. If the measurement is the same both vertically and horizontally, the house has settled and can be patched. Repair brick with mortar; repair concrete with patching cement. First clean out crumbled material with a screwdriver, so that the compound will not fall out (see Ortho's book, *Basic Home Repairs*).

2. Water damage: Look for signs of efflorescence—whitish, powdery mineral salt deposits pushed to the surface by moisture in the bricks or concrete. First try to discover and repair the source of the moisture (cracks or holes in the wall itself, leaky pipes, or damaged tiles in a bathroom or kitchen). Then brush off the deposits with a wire brush and muriatic acid (available at hardware stores). Follow the instructions on the label exactly—muriatic acid is a corrosive poison.

3. Spalling on brick walls: Spalling is the result of in-ternal pressures, or bricks soaking up water and then chipping apart when they freeze. Replace affected bricks and mortar (see Ortho's book, *Basic Home Repairs*), and then coat the entire wall with brick sealer (available at hardware stores and home-improvement centers).

Stucco

Ortho's book, *Basic Home Repairs*, gives specific instructions on repairing large and small holes and cracks in stucco.

Vinyl

Vinyl can become brittle and can crack if it's hit hard enough in very cold weather. Replace damaged sections with new boards. Repair small cracks and gaps between the siding and the wall with flexible vinyl siding caulk.

Wood

Commonly used wood sidings include clapboard planks, plywood panels, shakes, and shingles. Check for:

1. Loose, rotting, or missing sections: Repair or replace damaged wood siding to prevent water damage to the structure underneath. Be certain that the support structure is not damaged, before repairing the siding. Try to locate the source of any moisture—cracks or holes in the wall itself, leaky pipes, or damaged tiles in a bathroom or kitchen wall.

2. Cracked or peeling paint: Repaint only if you're certain the wood is sound. Painting rotten wood will only seal in the problems and cause the wood to deteriorate more rapidly. To prepare the surface, brush off loose paint with a wire brush and sand it smooth.

3. Rusty nails: This condition could indicate water damage and rot, or it may mean only that the original nails were not rustproof. Replace rusty nails with rust-proof ones to prevent dark streaks on the siding.

4. Signs of insects: Check for clusters of holes, tunnels, piles of fine sawdust, or discarded wings in the fall and spring. To eliminate insects, see Pests, pages 66–69.

Doors and windows

Even a small crack in a window will make the window more vulnerable to breaks. It should be replaced *or* painted with a commercial glass repair glue (available at hardware stores).

1. Broken glass: See Ortho's book, *Basic Home Repairs*, for instructions on replacing glass.

2. Rusty metal frames: Try to catch rust as soon as it appears—it will eventually oxidize the entire frame. Remove the rust with a wire brush, sandpaper, or a commercial rust remover/retardant (available at hardware and home-improvement stores). Paint the frames with a paint made especially for metal.

3. Gaps: Caulk gaps between frames or sills and siding to weatherproof and prevent water damage. See Ortho's book, *Energy Saving Projects for the Home*.

4. Screens, storm doors, and storm windows: Tighten loose frames with corrugated fasteners (available at hardware stores). If the screening or plastic is damaged,

Cleaning Windows Professionally

1. Spray the window with window cleaner or wipe it with a wet sponge.
2. Hold the squeegee at a 45-degree angle, and wipe the first inch at the top of the window. Then wipe off the squeegee blade.

3. Hold the squeegee at a 90-degree angle, and pull down from the top, overlapping each section slightly. Wipe the blade after each pass.
3a. On larger windows, pull in a continuous side-to-side motion.
4. Flick off any drops with your cloth.

---

some hardware stores will replace it for a reasonable price. To do it yourself, see Ortho's book, *Basic Home Repairs*. Lubricate the screen hinges if necessary, and patch peeling paint.

5. Painted frames and sills: If the paint is cracking or peeling, brush off the loose particles with a wire brush. Then sand smooth, and repaint. Water eventually will damage unpainted or unsealed wood.

Cleaning the exterior

To lengthen the life of your siding and put off an expensive repainting job, periodically remove the dirt and grime from painted and vinyl siding. It's not difficult, but it is time consuming, and you may want to hire a maintenance or janitorial professional to do it. Make certain the contractor is licensed and insured. Ask for an estimate and for names of clients you can call for an opinion of previous work. To do the work yourself, follow these step-by-step procedures.

1. Block all openings: Block dryer vents and plumbing pipe exits with newspaper or plastic sheeting. Close the doors and windows on sheets of newspaper to absorb any water that may seep underneath. Cover plants near the house to protect them from the water and detergent

you will be using. You will probably get wet, so dress appropriately.

2. Assemble your equipment: If the walls and eaves are especially dirty, rent a pressure washer from a rental supply store. Follow the manufacturer's instructions. *Or* use a bucket full of water and laundry detergent *or* an all-purpose cleaning liquid. You will also need rubber gloves, a brush (preferably with a long handle to help you reach the eaves), hoses long enough to reach all parts of the house, and a ladder. See Ortho's book *Basic Home Repairs* for guidelines on using ladders safely.

3. Wet one side: Spray one side of the house with the highest water pressure from your hose, washing off as much grime as you can. Spray the eaves, the area behind downspouts, the window sills, and around window and door frames. Roll out awnings to their most open position, and spray inside and out. Choose a day that is warm enough for them to dry quickly; otherwise they may mildew. Wet the areas that are still dirty with the cleaning solution, and leave it on while you move to the next side of the house. After spraying the second side and applying the cleaning solution, return to the first side and scrub off the dirt with a brush. Then rinse with the hose. Continue around the house until all sides are cleaned.

GARAGES

You probably think of your garage as a place for the car, as extra storage space, and perhaps as a workshop. But fire inspectors see garages as vulnerable fire areas; building inspectors check the garage first for signs of insects, moisture, and wood rot damage. The garage is also a common place for all kinds of household accidents, especially if you use it as a workshop. You should periodically check the roof, walls, doors, floors, foundations, appliances, and energy systems in your garage just like you check the rest of your house. Note the following guidelines for a garage inspection.

Storage

1. Check storage areas for combustibles (newspapers, charcoal starter, paint thinners), and flammables (gasoline, linseed oil, acetone). Be especially thorough around appliances, your hot water heater, and heating and cooling systems. Throw away what you can do without, or store these materials away from heat sources in approved metal containers with tight-fitting lids. In most states, it is illegal to store more than one gallon of gasoline (gasoline is the most explosive flammable in your house).

2. If your garage has an enclosed attic, check the stored items for fire hazards, and make certain that the access hatch is in place. Keep it closed—if there is a fire, the opening will act as a flue, drawing the flames to the roof.

3. Check the overhead storage racks to determine their security. If necessary, add extra bracing to keep them from falling.

Doors

1. The door leading into the house should be at least one step up to keep out heavier-than-air gasoline and oil fumes. Make certain the door is kept closed and is airtight. Seal with rubber weatherstripping and install a self-closing mechanism, *or* replace the hinges with spring-loaded self-closing types. Make sure that the door is solid. Sheet metal on a hollow-core door is not fire safe—in fact it helps conduct heat to the thin plywood.

2. There are two main types of outside garage doors—the swing-up type mounted on hinges, and the roll-up type with vertical tracks. Use powdered graphite to lubricate the roller(s) that sit inside the track. Check the track for bends, and straighten them with a hammer and wood block. Tighten the hinge screws and reinforcing rod. If the swing-type door sags, install a diagonal reinforcing rod. An overhead door that falls rapidly and heavily is a danger to pets and small children. Adjust the spring so that it closes with a slight push and comes down slowly. The springs on these doors can be hazardous if they break suddenly. Replace them with springs that include security rods (see illustration). Make certain the path is kept clear for an automatic garage door to swing open. Check the doors for weatherproofing. A drafty garage attached to the house is a major source of energy loss. To install weatherstripping, see Ortho's book, *Energy-Saving Projects for the Home*. For instructions on repairing and adjusting garage doors, see Ortho's book, *Basic Home Repairs*. If your garage door also has an entrance door in it, weatherstrip the entrance as well.

Roll-up (Vertical Track) Garage Door

Older garage door springs may break off and ricochet through the garage with great force. Replace such a spring with one that has a safety bar built into it. The safety

Swing-up Garage Door

bar will keep the spring attached to the door. If your door has an automatic opener, make sure cars and other objects are kept well away from its path.

Walls

1. Check all exposed wood for signs of dry rot—a puffy, reddish, musty-smelling fungus that deteriorates wood from the inside out. Replace affected timber. See pages 74–75 for more information on dry rot.

2. Check for signs of insects—mud termite tubes running up the walls, on pipes, or behind storage spaces; clusters of holes and/or piles of fine sawdust. See page 68 for more information.

3. Because exposed wood walls are a fire hazard, they should be covered with plaster, stucco, or wallboard.

4. To reduce heat loss from the house, insulate garage, walls, doors, and ceilings next to living spaces, and cover with a fire-retardant covering—plaster, stucco, or wallboard.

Floors

See page 27 for information on concrete floors.

Gas and electricity

1. All outlets should be grounded to prevent shocks. See pages 82–83 for more information.

2. In a heated garage, block air-return ducts leading to the house. If at all possible, find an alternative heating system. Do not let noxious fumes from the garage circulate back into the house.

3. Pilot lights and heating elements in hot water heaters, appliances, and heating and cooling systems must be 16 to 24 inches above the garage floor to prevent flammable, heavier-than-air fumes from coming into contact with them. Also, keep them well away from exposed wood walls. Call your local building inspector for the specific code restrictions in your area.

4. Exploding gas appliances are a common source of home fires. If you smell gas in the garage and you can't find and eliminate the problem, get out of the house immediately and call the fire department or your service company.

5. To check the general operating condition of your heating and cooling systems and electrical and plumbing systems, see pages 86–87 (heating and cooling), pages 82–83 (electrical), and pages 84–85 (plumbing).

Plumbing

1. Look for a pit in the floor covered with a metal plate. This may be a sewage clean-out, your house waste-line trap, or a water inlet pipe and turn-off. If the wood that was used to frame the floor when the concrete originally was laid is still in place, remove it if you can—it is an ideal place for an insect colony.

2. Insulate all exposed water pipes to keep them from freezing (insulation is available at hardware stores and home-improvement centers).

3. Your garage floor should slope toward a drainage hole to let water from a wet car run off. Otherwise, the moisture may damage wood and stored items, and rust metal. Cut down the amount of moisture in the garage by improving ventilation: Keep garage windows slightly open, or add vents along the bottom of the outside doors or walls.

Garage Safety

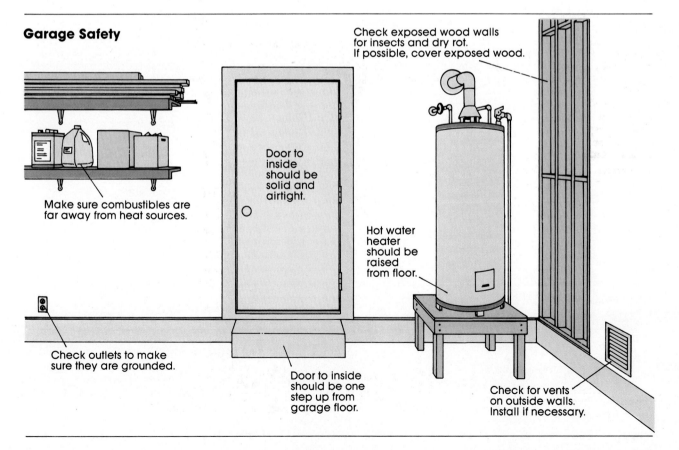

Check exposed wood walls for insects and dry rot. If possible, cover exposed wood.

Door to inside should be solid and airtight.

Hot water heater should be raised from floor.

Make sure combustibles are far away from heat sources.

Check outlets to make sure they are grounded.

Door to inside should be one step up from garage floor.

Check for vents on outside walls. Install if necessary.

ELECTRICAL SYSTEMS

You should know some basics about how any electrical system operates. You should also be familiar with the particular system in your home to be certain that it is well constructed, safe, and adequately supplying your needs. For instructions on how to make electrical repairs and how to install indoor and outdoor circuits and wiring, see Ortho's books, *Basic Home Repairs* and *Basic Wiring Techniques*. The following will help you check the safety of your system.

Wiring

Most wires through which electrical current passes are made of all copper, copper-clad aluminum, or pure aluminum. Some homes—especially those built between about 1964 and 1973—were wired with pure aluminum to beat the rising cost of copper. Both copper and copper-clad aluminum are safe for wiring purposes; however, pure aluminum, if improperly hooked to an outlet or switch, can cause fires or fatal shock. To check the wiring materials in your home, find some wiring that is exposed to view—in the attic or basement—and check how it is marked (all-aluminum is stamped "AL" or "ALUMINUM"). If you have any doubts about its safety, check with a licensed electrician. If you discover old-fashioned knob and tube wiring, inspect it for frayed or cracked insulation. This too can be a dangerous situation—have it inspected for safety by a licensed electrician.

Service boxes

You should know where your fuse or circuit breaker box is in case you ever need to shut off the main supply of electricity, switch a circuit breaker back on, or change a fuse. Whenever a fuse blows, determine why it happened so the same thing doesn't happen again. Short circuits can mean faulty wiring, which is a fire hazard.

The most common problem is overload—too many appliances being used at the same time. If you suspect an overload, take some of the load off before you replace the fuse or flip the switch back on. If you suspect a short circuit and you can't find the cause, call an electrician before replacing the fuse or flipping the switch back on. Put labels on your fuse box or circuit breaker box to indicate which fuse handles which circuit. This will help you to pinpoint future problems quickly, especially in an emergency. The following list indicates types of service boxes and explains how to restore power after a circuit has been interrupted or a fuse has blown:

Cartridge fuse: Turn off the main power supply, pull out the removable plate, and remove the fuses with a cartridge fuse remover. You can't see a melted metal link in a blown cartridge—use a continuity tester to determine which fuse is affected. Correct the source of the problem, then replace with a new cartridge fuse.

Circuit breaker: Circuit breakers trip or turn off automatically when there is an overload or short. Determine the source of the problem and correct it. Then push the lever all the way off, and reset the switch to "on."

Plug- or Edison-base fuse: If the metal link is broken, the fuse has been overloaded. Blackened glass usually indicates a short circuit. Turn off the main power supply, unscrew the damaged fuse, and replace it with one of the same amperage. Touch only the glass while making the exchange. If you are constantly replacing plug fuses because of overloads, try replacing them with breaker fuses instead—the button will pop out and cut off the circuit instead of breaking the link.

Type-S or nontamperable fuse: These fuses screw into an adapter in the socket so that you cannot install a fuse with a higher amp rating than the circuit can safely bear. Check and replace them in the same way as plug fuses.

Types of Fuses

Testing a Fuse with a Continuity Tester

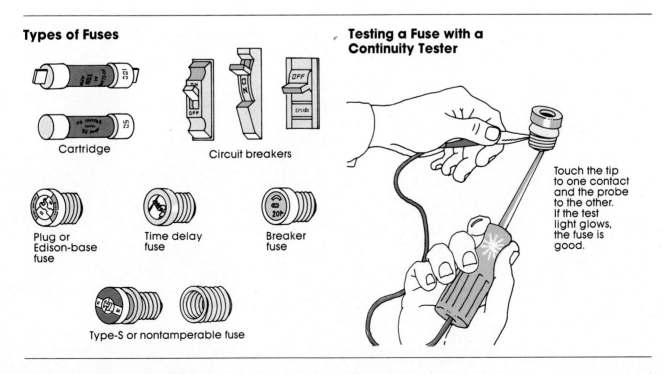

Cartridge

Circuit breakers

Plug or Edison-base fuse

Time delay fuse

Breaker fuse

Type-S or nontamperable fuse

Touch the tip to one contact and the probe to the other. If the test light glows, the fuse is good.

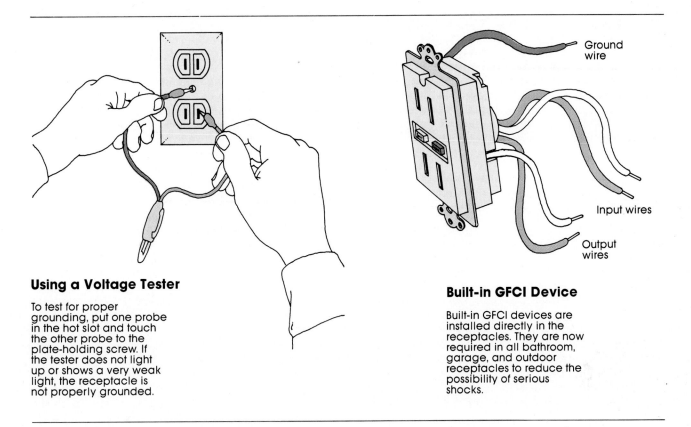

Using a Voltage Tester

To test for proper grounding, put one probe in the hot slot and touch the other probe to the plate-holding screw. If the tester does not light up or shows a very weak light, the receptacle is not properly grounded.

Built-in GFCI Device

Built-in GFCI devices are installed directly in the receptacles. They are now required in all bathroom, garage, and outdoor receptacles to reduce the possibility of serious shocks.

Overloads and short circuits

When more electricity flows through the fuses and wires than they can carry, the system overloads and shuts down on that circuit. When two wires touch, they fuse together from the heat generated, and the flow of current is interrupted. Check the following list to determine the cause of these common electrical problems.

1. If a fuse blows almost immediately after you plug something in, regardless of what circuit you try, that indicates a short in the appliance, lamp, or tool itself. Unplug it and check the connection near the plug and where it meets the appliance, lamp, or tool. The problem is commonly in the cord, where two wires have touched. Replace the damaged plug or wiring.

2. If a fuse routinely blows on one circuit, it is probably a simple overload. You will have to use fewer lights, appliances, and tools on that circuit. *Or,* consult an electrician about increasing your electrical service capacity.

3. If a fuse blows when you start up an electric motor in your workshop, you might be able to correct the problem by using a time-delay fuse (see illustration). This handles the temporary overload required to start the motor. But if the problem persists, check for a short circuit in the motor, plug, or cord.

4. If a fuse has blown and an outlet no longer works, there may be a short in the hidden wiring. Have this checked by a licensed electrician.

Grounding

If your system is grounded, leaking electrical current from a short or loose wires will be directed into the ground

through a copper wire connected to a water pipe or a rod buried in the ground. Most local codes now require further grounding protection. See Ortho's book, *Basic Wiring Techniques,* for an update on the grounding electrode system. Check the following to determine whether (and, if so, how) your system is grounded.

Outlets: Check your outlets for two slits and a hole in the receptacle. If they have slits only, there may still be a grounding wire. Test with a circuit tester to confirm grounding (see illustration). To plug three-pronged plugs into a two-slit, grounded outlet, use an adapter plug with a pigtail that attaches to the center screw. If the outlets are not grounded, especially in areas where there is water, consult a licensed electrician for alternative safety measures.

Ground fault circuit interrupters: These devices to monitor current flow are installed in an outlet or the service panel. If there is even a tiny discrepancy (a drop in the returning current when someone receives even a mild shock, for instance), it shuts off all current on that circuit in about a fortieth of a second. These devices are now required in all bathrooms and outdoor wiring. They could be included for extra safety, but are not required in kitchen, laundry, and workshop circuits.

Appliances and power tools: Most recently made appliances and tools are double insulated, so that if a wire inside should short out or become loose, it will not be conducted to you through the metal or plastic body. If you have older-model tools and appliances, check that they have three-pronged plugs and that the cords are in good shape, and plug them into grounded outlets only.

PLUMBING SYSTEMS

In an emergency, you and your family should know how to find and operate water supply valves, how to quickly plug a sudden leak in a pipe, and how to unclog your sink or toilet. If flooding water comes into contact with your electrical system, a real hazard can result. If there is standing water, be sure to turn off all the power to the house before you make any repairs to the plumbing or electrical systems. Detailed instructions on how to repair pipes, toilets, and faucets appear in Ortho's books, *Basic Home Repairs* and *Basic Plumbing Techniques*.

Shutoff valves

Before an emergency ever arises, you can do a few things to minimize damage and make any problem easier to handle. Learn where all the water and gas shutoff valves are, and make sure they are operable. In some areas, the main water valve may be operable only by the water company. The valve may require a special tool or it may be padlocked. In emergencies, you'll need to turn off the individual shutoff valves instead of the main. The main water valve should be somewhere between the water meter and your house. Usually it's either near the meter or near the main water line where it enters the house. In cold-weather areas, the meter may be in the basement or crawlspace, and you will probably find the main valve very close to the meter. If the plumbing in your house has been properly designed and installed, you should need to use the main water valve only on rare occasions. In most situations, the individual shutoff valves will do.

Each fixture or appliance that uses water should have a shutoff valve for each pipe carrying water to it: usually, one for the cold water and one for the hot. You will find these valves under sinks and toilet tanks, on top of the water heater, and behind washing machines and dishwashers. Many codes require separate valves for each fixture: you rarely find them on showers or tubs. Some plumbing systems have additional shutoff valves where branch lines leave the main line to serve the various parts of the house. Find your shutoff valves. If it's not obvious which part of the system is served by each valve, turn one off and check to see what doesn't work. Then label the valve so you won't waste time in an emergency. Always turn valves clockwise to shut them off. The illustration on the right shows where you are likely to find shutoff valves.

Drain systems

Used water and waste are separated from your incoming system, and drain by gravity flow. Vent pipes are connected to the system to carry off excess gases. At each fixture, the drain pipes contain a U- or S-shaped vent called a trap. The trap retains water and acts as a seal to prevent gases, bacteria, and vermin from entering the house. Each run of most drainage pipes ends with a cleanout for access to the system. Look for them near the foundation or in the basement, and make certain they are tightly capped. The diagram on the facing page shows where you are likely to find your drain traps, cleanouts, and vent pipes. Check your attic—vent pipes terminating in the attic are in violation of plumbing codes.

Routine care

Sinks and tubs: To prevent clogs, use a strainer to keep hair and solid matter out of the drain. Clean it out regularly. Grease should never be poured down the drain; instead, pour it into a disposable container. To prevent clogs, pour a solution of vinegar and washing soda *or* baking soda down drains once a week. For dripping faucets, have an assortment of washers on hand.

Toilets: Keep disposable diapers and such out of the toilet. Never use the toilet to dispose of garbage.

Pipes: Insulate pipes to keep them from freezing, or from dripping due to condensation. Special insulation for pipes is available at hardware stores.

Hot water heaters: Check the following tips for care.

1. Every two months or so, drain off a dishpan full of water. This keeps the sediment from building up on the bottom and reducing the unit's heating efficiency.

2. Once a year, push down or up on the pressure relief valve to make sure it's working. The valve is connected to an overflow pipe so that if water is forced out it won't spray all over the room. Ortho's book, *Basic Home Repairs*, describes how to install a valve.

3. About once a year, in hard-water areas, have the hot water tank de-limed and cleaned by a trained service person.

4. Set the thermostat between 120° and 160°F. If it is electric, there may be two thermostats to adjust. These are located behind the controls. The lower temperature setting will save you money.

5. Insulate the tank and pipes (materials are available from most hardware stores and home-improvement centers). By maintaining the temperature of hot water for a longer period and preventing rusty pipes from condensation, you will save money on heating bills.

6. Every two years, clean the chimney in gas or oil heaters. Call your water company for a recommended professional *or* for instructions to do the job yourself.

Special problems

Leaks: Repairs of exposed leaky pipes are discussed in Ortho's books, *Basic Home Repairs* and *Basic Plumbing Techniques*. Fixing concealed pipes may be best left to a professional.

Clogs: If the toilet, sink, tub, or shower won't drain:

1. Plug the overflow opening with a wet rag.

2. Push a plunger firmly into the drain hole, working it up and down rapidly.

3. If that doesn't work, add water to keep it more than half full, then try again. Do not attempt to flush the toilet until it begins to drain.

4. If it is still clogged, use a drain chemical. Follow the instructions on the label very carefully—most drain chemicals are corrosive and toxic.

Overflowing: If your dishwasher or clothes washer overflows, turn off the shutoff valve behind the appliance. If you can't reach it, shut the water off at the hot water heater or the main shutoff valve. Check the drain for lint, grease, or dirt, and clean it out. If the water keeps flowing after the controls indicate it is off, turn off the electricity to that circuit and pull the plug. The timer or electrical system on the appliance may be at fault and must be repaired by a professional. If the water continues to flow after you turn the water back on, turn the water off and call a plumber; or see Ortho's book, *Basic Plumbing Techniques.*

Low water pressure: If the water pressure in your home is too low to handle your needs, there are several possible causes and solutions. The shutoff valves may not be completely open. Check them all, and open them as far as you can. The pipes may be partially blocked with deposits or debris. A thorough cleanout—manually or with a chemical—may solve the problem. See Ortho's book, *Basic Plumbing Techniques,* for instructions. If the pipes are corroded, corroded material may be blocking them. They will eventually leak and have to be replaced. Check the main incoming pipe for a water pressure valve—you may not have one. If you do, it may have been partially closed to reduce the amount of water used by the previous owner or tenant. As a last resort, call a professional to help you determine how to increase your water supply.

See Ortho's books, *Basic Home Repairs* and *Basic Plumbing Techniques,* for instructions on how to repair hot water heaters, noisy pipes, and frozen pipes.

Finding Water Supply Valves

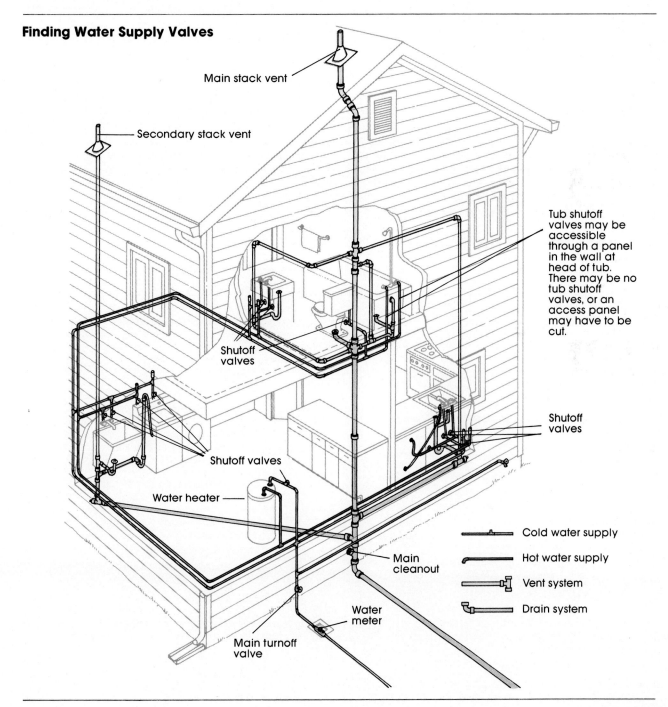

Main stack vent

Secondary stack vent

Tub shutoff valves may be accessible through a panel in the wall at head of tub. There may be no tub shutoff valves, or an access panel may have to be cut.

Shutoff valves

Shutoff valves

Shutoff valves

Water heater

Main cleanout

Water meter

Main turnoff valve

Cold water supply

Hot water supply

Vent system

Drain system

HEATING & COOLING SYSTEMS

Heating systems

Maintaining any heating or cooling system requires an understanding of its basic components and how the system operates. If you have no written material or manuals, hire an insured professional to check and service your system. Ask him to explain how it works, which problems you can fix yourself, what parts you will need (filter size, for example), and where you can find them. This basic understanding of your particular system will show you how logical and straightforward most systems are and how easy they are to maintain. Well-maintained systems will save you hundreds of energy dollars each year. For diagrams of specific systems and some of the more complicated repairs you can do yourself, see Ortho's book, *Energy-Saving Projects for the Home*. The following list deals with components common to many types of heating systems.

Filters: A dusty or dirty filter will retard the passage of air and make your blower and burners work harder than necessary. In the early fall and at least once a month during the cold weather season, clean or replace the filter. If you live in a dusty area or your heater is on most of the time, clean or change the filter once a month.

Registers or grilles: If dust or dirt accumulates in the ducts below the registers or grilles, you may notice unfamiliar odors each time you turn on the heat. Vacuum them regularly, and check periodically to make sure no objects or debris have fallen through the grates. Don't block them with draperies or furniture—they lower the efficiency of the system by interrupting the flow of air.

Ducts and pipes: Gaps or leaks in the ducts will keep you from receiving all the heat your system is generating. Turn on the fan or blower, and run your hand along any exposed ducts. (See illustration below). To prevent an expensive plumbing job, check exposed pipes in radiant, steam, or hot water system for rust or leaks. Repair as described in Ortho's book, *Basic Plumbing* Techniques.

Thermostats: To ensure that your thermostat is sending the correct message to your heater, check it for accuracy. Tape a wood-backed thermometer on the wall next to the thermostat. After an hour see if the heater turns on when the thermometer registers the same temperature as the thermostat setting. If not, clean and adjust as decribed in Ortho's book, *Basic Home Repairs*.

Fans and blowers: If your fan or blower is noisy, it may be off balance because it is covered with grime. Turn off the power to that circuit and clean the blades with soap and water. Avoid dripping the solution onto the motor. If the fan or blower is especially dirty or you can't reach it, ask your service inspector to remove and clean it. If you hear squeaks and your blower or fan takes a long time to start up, it may need oiling. If so, follow this procedure: Turn off the power to that circuit. Squeeze a few drops of No. 10 nondetergent motor oil into each oil port on the motor, and on the fan or blower. Also oil the shaft between the blower or fan and the motor.

Pilot lights: Turn your pilot lights off during the summer months to save energy and reduce residual heat; remember that whenever you use combustible materials, such as paint thinners, the heavier-than-air fumes may build up along the floor and be ignited by the pilot light.

Replacing Furnace Filters

1. Turn off thermostat.

2. Locate metal panel that covers the filter, near the blower.

3. Remove panel and slide filter out.

4. Slide new filter in, according to air-flow directions on the filter.

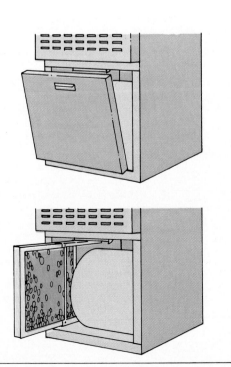

Plugging Leaks and Saving Heat

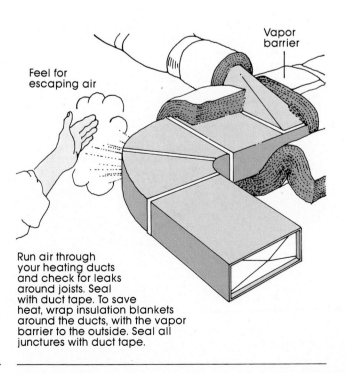

Feel for escaping air

Vapor barrier

Run air through your heating ducts and check for leaks around joists. Seal with duct tape. To save heat, wrap insulation blankets around the ducts, with the vapor barrier to the outside. Seal all junctures with duct tape.

Maintaining a Room Air Conditioner

1. Unplug the unit before working on it.

2. At beginning of cooling season and then as often as every few weeks, change or clean filter. Remove front panel and filter. Wash filter in mild detergent, rinse, dry, and replace. Be careful not to tear it.

3. Clean condensor coil fins with vacuum cleaner or brush. Straighten bent fins with a fin comb.

4. Make sure plug is not frayed.

5. Do not touch capacitor. Electricity is stored here, and you can get a shock even when the unit is unplugged.

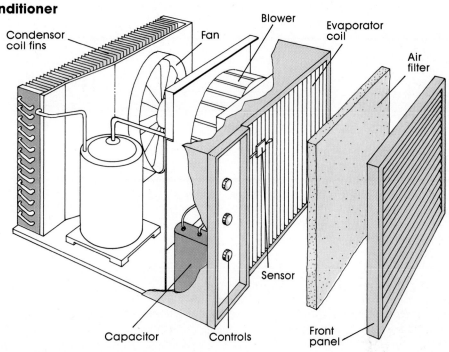

Condensor coil fins — Fan — Blower — Evaporator coil — Air filter — Sensor — Capacitor — Controls — Front panel

---

Most gas heating systems include detailed instructions on the control panel for relighting pilot lights.

Follow those instructions carefully. If you're in doubt about any part of the procedure, call a professional. If you suspect a gas leak from the pilot light or from any other source, don't try to correct it yourself. Get out of the house quickly, leaving a door open, and call your service company or the fire department immediately.

Boilers: Mineral deposits and sediment eventually will corrode the boiler housing and cause leaks. They also reduce your heater's efficiency by insulating the boiler from the heat source. Drain a gallon or two from the boiler at least once a month during the heating season. Turn off the thermostat; let the water cool, then drain it into a bucket.

Radiators: Because a radiator literally radiates heat through exposed pipes, it's important to keep the surfaces free of dust or dirt. Clean off the radiator with the brush attachment when you vacuum. If it's very dirty, place damp newspapers underneath, and clean with a radiator brush. Radiators can also fill with air and reduce the amount of heat available to you. Release the air through the flow-control valve two or three times a year. Wait until the radiator is cold so that hot water doesn't spurt out and scald you. Hold a cup or pail under the valve to catch the water. Open the valve until water begins to flow out, then close it quickly.

Air conditioners

To find out how to maintain your air conditioner on your own, talk to your dealer or service person. Here are some general instructions for cleaning and checking your system.

1. If you can reach them, clean central air conditioner's condenser coils, or have your serviceman clean them during your annual maintenance check. Turn off the power to that circuit, and reverse your vacuum cleaner to blow the dirt away. Do not touch the air conditioner with the metal hose.

2. Clean and replace air filters every month or two, depending on the frequency and intensity with which you use the unit.

3. To reduce the air conditioner's fuel waste, provide some shade or cover for the condenser outside. Make sure that trees, fences, or bushes do not block the passage of air into or around the condenser.

4. If your heating and cooling systems use the same ducts, adjust the dampers each time you change from one system to the other, since each requires a different setting. Consult your dealer, manual, or service person.

Fireplaces and wood stoves

Check your fireplace or wood stove periodically for fire safety. Most chimney and wood stove fires start in the flue, where soot and creosote build up, and can be ignited by a single spark. Creosote is a shiny, black, tarlike deposit that reflects light; soot is dull, black, and powdery. Because it clings to the flammable creosote, you may have to knock off the soot to discover the creosote. If the buildup is ¼-inch thick or more, clean the flue before building another fire. Clean at least once a year, before or after the cold-weather season. If you have fires more than five days a week, clean the flue once in the middle of the season as well. To inspect the exterior chimney, see Chimneys, page 77. Inspect and clean your fireplace, woodstove, or free-standing fireplace as follows.

Fireplace Flue

You can clean the flue yourself, but it's a good idea to hire a licensed and insured professional the first time to see how it's done. Look in the Yellow Pages under "Chimney Sweeps."

Dampers: When the fireplace is not in use, close the damper to keep out drafts. To ensure proper air movement to the chimney, clean the damper once or twice a year. Wear goggles and gloves to keep the soot out of your eyes and protect your hands. Scrub with a wire brush. Oil the rod at both ends of the damper to make it easier to open and close. Clean the smoke shelf at the same time.

Firebox: A clean, empty fireplace during the spring and summer is much more attractive than an ash-filled one. Use a dustpan to clean out all the ashes at the end of the burning season. Make certain there are no sparks or embers. Use a metal dustpan, and dispose of the ashes in a metal container. Use a brush and hot, soapy water to scrub the firebox. During the season, remove only the excess ashes—fires light and burn better if you build them on an inch or two of ashes.

Brick or stone facing: You may be able to prevent smoke stains on the outside of your fireplace by raising the height of your fire. Add a layer or two of fire brick to the firebox floor. If it helps, install it permanently. To clean brick, metal, or stone, see Household Items, pages 52–61.

Woodstoves

Although there are many different kinds of wood- and coal-burning stoves and freestanding fireplaces, their maintenance, repair, and safety considerations are similar. In some states, wood stoves are the third most frequent cause of fire—mostly from incorrect installation and maintenance. Ask any woodstove or freestanding fireplace dealer for the National Safety Guidelines and Codes. Read them carefully and check your stove, flue, chimney, stack, and floor- and wall-fireproofing. If they do not meet the codes, they are hazardous and should be brought up to code before you build another fire. Don't use your stove or fireplace to burn trash or magazines—this causes excessive creosote and soot, and may release chemicals and fumes that are noxious or toxic. Pressed logs should not be used in open woodstoves or freestanding fireplaces—they are impregnated with wax and shoot off sparks. Inspect and clean your woodstove or freestanding fireplace as follows.

Stovepipe: If you have a metal stack that goes through the roof, make certain it is grounded. Look for a wire running to an outside plumbing pipe or a rod in the ground. If not, it can act as a lightning rod. Clean it twice a year or more, following these steps:

1. Label the sections so you can reassemble them correctly.
2. Spread newspaper on the stove and floor to keep them clean.
3. Disassemble the pipe, and carry it outside in a large plastic bag.
4. Clean the inside of the pipe with crumpled newspaper or a flue brush. Use a wire brush for thick creosote buildup.

Cleaning the Flue

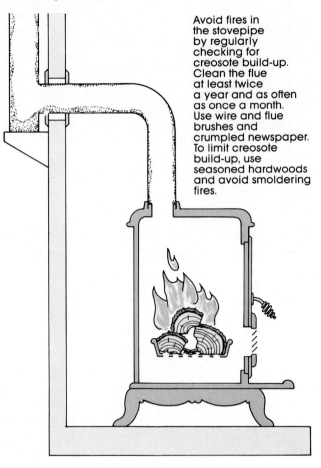

Avoid fires in the stovepipe by regularly checking for creosote build-up. Clean the flue at least twice a year and as often as once a month. Use wire and flue brushes and crumpled newspaper. To limit creosote build-up, use seasoned hardwoods and avoid smoldering fires.

5. Reassemble the pipe, and replace it on the stove.

Firebox: Remove the grate, if there is one, and clean out the ashes or sand so you can clean and inspect as follows:

1. Use a wire brush to clean off the creosote and soot from the walls.
2. Remove the baffle system if you can, and clean it with a wire brush. If it's not removable, clean it in place.
3. Check the metal for cracks, and repair with stove cement (available at hardware stores and home-improvement centers). Even a small crack decreases the efficiency of a tightly sealed stove or fireplace.
4. Check the seal on the door. A cracked or broken seal will greatly reduce the efficiency of a sealed unit. Replace it, if necessary, with one the same size (available from your stove dealer or the manufacturer).
5. Replace crumbling fire bricks (available from larger nurseries and some lumberyards) to keep your unit from getting too hot on the outside.
6. Replace the grates and sand.

Exterior surface: Keep up the appearance of your cast iron stove and protect it from rust by coating it once a year with stove blacking (available at hardward stores and home improvement centers). Follow label directions. To clean other types of metal stoves, consult your local dealer, and check the Metals chart on page 61.

DRIVEWAYS, WALKS & PATIOS

Grass and weeds will loosen paving stones and bricks, and enlarge cracks in concrete and asphalt. Pull out the unwanted growth, and pour hot salt water or weed killer on these areas to prevent the weeds from returning. If not repaired as soon as you notice them, small cracks, potholes, and loose paving stones can develop into a major repair expense, or cause someone to twist an ankle. (Materials needed for these repairs are available at most hardware stores and home improvement centers.) Follow the guidelines below for making repairs.

Blacktop: Protect blacktop against weather damage by covering it with blacktop sealer. See Ortho's book, *Basic Home Repairs,* for instructions. Blacktop is prone to drying out and cracking. Brush loose matter out of small cracks and fill the cracks with butyl cement. Smooth the top with a putty knife. Fill large cracks and holes with blacktop patching compound, packing it down with a shovel. Lay a board on top of the area, and drive over it with your car to compact it completely. See illustration below.

Brick: Repair cracks in bricks and mortar as discussed in Exterior Walls, pages 78–79, and in Ortho's book, *Basic*

Home Repairs. Some walks and patios are made by laying bricks on top of a layer of sand, and filling the cracks with sand or dirt. If they become loosened by rain or hosing, simply smooth the sand underneath and refill the cracks.

Concrete: Cracks and holes are usually caused by the ground underneath eroding or settling. For small repairs, use ready-to-mix cement containing a bonding agent. For larger areas, it's cheaper to buy the concrete and a small can of bonding agent separately. Follow the instructions on the package to mix the two, and see Ortho's book, *Basic Home Repairs,* for instructions.

Gravel or crushed stone: If your driveway or walk is on a slope, water or cars may cause gravel and crushed stone to slide towards the bottom. Rake it back into place, and line the edges with boards to help keep it from sliding again.

Stone: Flagstone is relatively easily split or chipped. When this happens, clean the pieces, coat each matching surface with epoxy resin, and fit them together. Wipe off the excess resin immediately. Weight flat until the join is dry.

Repairing Holes in Blacktop

1. Chip away loose asphalt.

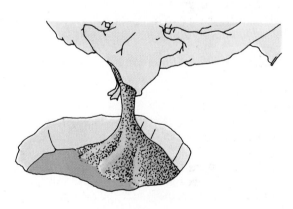

2. Pour in patching compound.

3. Tamp down with back of shovel.

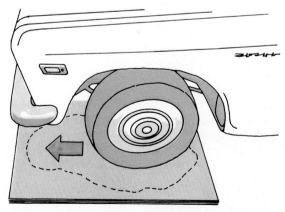

4. Drive car over patch covered with plywood.

DECKS & POOLS

Decks

Wood is prone to rot, especially outside. It is much easier to prevent rot than to replace damaged wood. If you're building a new deck, use naturally rot-resistant wood, or wood that has been treated with water repellants or preservatives. Check your existing deck for rot and other problems:

1. Poke into the wood with an ice-pick, especially around joints, railings, braces, support poles, and the ends of boards. If the wood is soft or crumbling, replace it with treated wood.

2. The joints between your deck and the house can loosen in time. Rescrew or renail loose wood and metal bracing with rust-proof nails or screws.

3. Diagonal bracing and poles must remain solid to continue to support the load of a deck. Check for security, and strengthen with screws, nails, and extra bracing.

4. Railings should be solidly attached to the deck. If they are loose or wobbly, renail or add extra bracing.

5. Weathered paint or stain can no longer protect wood from rot. Keep the wood protected by renewing the finish, as needed.

Pools

Whether your pool is plaster-coated concrete, fiberglass, gunite, or vinyl-lined, maintaining its systems and keeping the water clean involves the same procedures.

Swimming-season maintenance

Some pool companies offer year-round maintenance of your water and systems for a set fee. Because pool maintenance can be a time-consuming job—8 to 10 hours a week at the height of the season—you may want to consider having it done professionally.

Daily

1. Skim leaves and debris from the surface of the water and the bottom of the pool.

2. Clean out strainer basket.

3. Check filter pressure, and clean out filter when water is no longer clear, following manufacturer's instructions.

Weekly

1. Test water with a water-test kit (available, with instructions, from a pool-supply store) and add the recommended chemicals.

2. Brush tile and walls with a nylon brush. Use a stainless steel brush to loosen algae on concrete and gunite walls.

3. Check walls or vinyl liner for cracks or tears, and repair. Use an underwater patching compound on concrete or gunite, a fiberglass repair kit on fiberglass, and a vinyl repair kit on vinyl (all available from pool-supply or hardware stores).

4. Hose off the deck, aiming the water away from the pool.

Winter maintenance

In mild-winter areas, continue your summer-season maintenance program on a reduced schedule, adding extra chlorine to help keep the water clear. Test the water, and clean out debris once a month. Run the filter pump about half as much as you do during the swimming season. A pool cover will greatly reduce the amount of maintenance your pool will require during the winter months. To winterize in severe-weather areas, follow the list below.

1. To clean out dirt and debris from the water, run the filter for several hours and vacuum it thoroughly.

2. Clean the filter according to manufacturer's instructions. Remove the cartridge from a cartridge-type filter and store it in a warm, dry place.

3. Lower the water level until you can reach the outlets, and empty all supply and return pipes and lines of as much water as possible. Plug the outlets with adjustable rubber plugs. Drain water from the heater, filter, and pump.

4. Add water to the natural water line, and put pool cover in place (see Ortho's book, *Energy-Saving Projects for the Home*).

5. Turn off all gas and electricity to the pool's systems.

Reopening the pool in spring

It's best to have a professional start your heater and pump, and test and treat the water at the beginning of the season. Before this person comes, hose off the deck and cover, and remove the plugs from the outlets.

The primary source of heat loss in a swimming pool is evaporation. A swimming pool cover reduces most of the evaporation, traps heat, and keeps debris out of the water. Of the wide variety of pool covers available, a simple hand-winch mechanism such as the one shown here, is easily installed and easy to operate. Electrically operated mechanisms are more expensive but even simpler to use. Whatever your choice, a pool cover is a sound investment.

LANDSCAPE MAINTENANCE

Winter

1. Plan vegetable and flower beds.

2. Order seeds and bare-root trees and shrubs (roses and fruit trees).

3. Prune roses, trees, and shrubs before spring growth begins. (For spring-flowering trees and shrubs, such as flowering fruit trees, prune as soon as the flowers drop in the spring.)

Spring

1. Spread pre-emergent herbicide.

2. Plant annual vegetables and flowers. Plant bare-root trees and shrubs as soon as you can work the soil.

3. Using a hoe or contact herbicide, kill weeds as soon as they appear. Careful control in the spring will help to keep the yard clean all year.

4. Fertilize lawns and plants as soon as vigorous growth begins.

5. Begin watering during dry spells.

6. Mulch to keep down weeds.

7. Shear hedges whenever they have about 4 inches of new growth, or when they begin to look ragged.

8. Watch for aphids. Spray as soon as they appear.

9. Check the garden weekly for insect or disease problems. Apply controls immediately.

Summer

1. Keep up the weed control to prevent weeds from going to seed.

2. Water whenever the soil a couple of inches under the surface is only a little moist. Leave the water on long enough to wet the soil as deep as the roots go.

3. Remove spent flowers to keep the garden looking neat.

4. If a tree is growing too fast (has too many water-sprouts), prune it in July instead of winter; this will slow its growth next spring.

5. Fertilize every 6 weeks as long as plants are growing. Cut down on fertilizer for cool-season lawns before hot weather arrives.

6. Shade heat-sensitive plants during heat waves to keep them from burning.

7. Take out summer annuals as soon as their peak season has passed. Replace them with cool-season flowers for fall color. In warm-winter areas, plant winter flowers and vegetables.

8. Continue watching for pests and diseases. Mites and powdery mildew become active during hot weather.

Fall

1. Rake fallen leaves every four days to keep them from turning the lawn yellow. Use some of the leaves as a mulch under shrubs and trees. If the leaves are large and soft, such as maple leaves, shred them first to keep them from compacting.

2. Clean out flower and vegetable beds as soon as they finish bearing. Till the beds and mulch them with leaves.

3. Feed cool-season lawns as soon as they begin growing rapidly when the weather turns cool. This is the season to aerate, level, and patch lawns.

The seasonal landscape maintenance calendar on this page will help you keep on top of your home gardening tasks.

4. Thatch warm-season lawns as soon as they become dormant.

5. In mild-winter areas, control weeds as soon as they appear.

6. As soon as leaves drop, spray deciduous trees and shrubs with a dormant oil spray to control overwintering insects.

7. Plant bulbs as soon as they arrive.

8. Clean, paint, and store garden furniture.

9. Mulch perennials to keep them from being heaved by repeated freezing and thawing of the soil.

10. If the fall has been dry, water well before the ground freezes.

11. Protect tender plants from cold and from winter drying.

INDEX

U.S. Measure and Metric Measure Conversion Chart

FORMULAS FOR EXACT MEASURE   **ROUNDED MEASURES FOR QUICK REFERENCE**

MASS (WEIGHT)

Symbol	When you know:	Multiply by:	To find:					
oz	ounces	28.35	grams	1 oz		=		30 g
lb	pounds	0.45	kilograms	4 oz		=		115 g
g	grams	0.035	ounces	8 oz		=		225 g
kg	kilograms	2.2	pounds	16 oz	=	1 lb	=	450 g
				32 oz	=	2 lb	=	900 g
				36 oz	=	2¼ lb	=	1000 g (1 kg)

VOLUME

Symbol	When you know:	Multiply by:	To find:					
tsp	teaspoons	5	milliliters	¼ tsp	=	1/24 oz	=	1 ml
tbsp	tablespoons	15	milliliters	½ tsp	=	1/12 oz	=	2 ml
fl oz	fluid ounces	29.57	milliliters	1 tsp	=	1/6 oz	=	5 ml
c	cups	0.24	liters	1 tbsp	=	½ oz	=	15 ml
pt	pints	0.47	liters	1 c	=	8 oz	=	250 ml
qt	quarts	0.95	liters	2 c (1 pt)	=	16 oz	=	500 ml
gal	gallons	3.785	liters	4 c (1 qt)	=	32 oz	=	1 l
ml	milliliters	0.034	fluid ounces	4 qt (1 gal)	=	128 oz	=	3¾ l

LENGTH

Symbol	When you know:	Multiply by:	To find:					
in.	inches	2.54	centimeters	⅜ in.		=		1 cm
ft	feet	30.48	centimeters	1 in.		=		2.5 cm
yd	yards	0.9144	meters	2 in.		=		5 cm
mi	miles	1.609	kilometers	2½ in.		=		6.5 cm
km	kilometers	.621	miles	12 in. (1 ft)		=		30 cm
m	meters	1.094	yards	1 yd		=		90 cm
cm	centimeters	0.39	inches	100 ft		=		30 m
				1 mi		=		1.6 km

TEMPERATURE

Symbol	When you know:	Multiply by:	To find:					
F°	Fahrenheit	5/9 (after subtracting 32)	Celsius	32° F		=		0° C
C°	Celsius	9/5 + 32	Fahrenheit	68° F		=		20° C
				212° F		=		100° C

AREA

Symbol	When you know:	Multiply by:	To find:					
in.^{2}	square inches	6.452	square centimeters	1 in.^{2}		=		6.5 cm^2
ft^2	square feet	929	square centimeters	1 ft^2		=		930 cm^2
yd^2	square yards	8631	square centimeters	1 yd^2		=		8360 cm^2
a	acres	.4047	hectares	1 a		=		4050 m^2

Manufacturers of major appliances and equipment

If you've lost your owner's manuals for any of your household appliances or equipment, you can write to the manufacturer for replacements. Be sure to include the model and serial numbers. This list represents some of the larger companies. Names and addresses of other companies are available at your local library.

Amana
Main St.
Amana, IA 52204
319/622-5511

Bissel
2345 Walker Rd., N.W.
Grand Rapids, MI 49504
616/453-4451

Braun
The Schawbel Corp.
281 Albany St.
Cambridge, MA 02139
617/492-2100

Cuisinart
411 W. Putnam Ave.
Greenwich, CT 06830
203/622-4608

Eureka
1201 E. Bell St.
Bloomington, IL 61701
309/828-2367

Hoover
101 E. Maple St.
No. Canton, OH 44720
216/499-9200

Farberware
Kidd Company
1500 Bassett Ave.
Bronx, NY 10461
212/863-8000

Frigidaire
General Motors Co.
P.O. Box 4900
Dayton, OH 45449
513/297-3400

General Electric
3135 Easton Turnpike
Fairfield, CT 06431
203/373-2211

Gibson
515 W. Gibson Dr.
Greenville, MI 48838
616/754-5621

Hamilton-Beach
P.O. Box 1158
Washington, NC 27889
919/946-6401

Kirby
1920 W. 114th St.
Cleveland, OH 44102
216/228-2400

Krups
Robert Krups
No. America
7 Pearl Ct.
Allendale, NJ 07401
201/825-1116

Maytag
403 W. 4th St., No.
Newton, IA 50208
515/792-7000

Mr. Coffee
North American
Systems, Inc.
Bedford Heights,
OH 44146
216/464-4000

Norelco
North American
Phillips Corp.
High Ridge Park
Stamford, CT 06904
203/329-5700

Norge
Herrin, IL 62948
618/988-8431

Oster
5055 N. Lydell Ave.
Milwaukee, WI 53217
414/332-8300

Panasonic
1 Panasonic Way
Secaucus, NJ 07094
201/348-7000

Proctor-Silex
1016-T W. 9th Ave.
King of Prussia, PA 19406
215/265-8000

Quasar
9401 W. Grand Ave.
Franklin Park, IL 60131
312/451-1200

Roper
1905 W. Court St.
Kankakee, IL 60901
815/927-6000

Speed Queen
Shepard & Hall Sts.
Ripon, WI 54971
414/748-3121

Sunbeam
5400 W. Roosevelt Rd.
Chicago, IL 60650
312/854-3500

Tappan
Tappan Park
Mansfield, OH 44901
419/529-4411

Toshiba
82 Totowa Rd.
Wayne, NJ 07470
201/628-8000

Waring
Route 44
Hartford, CT 06057
203/379-0731

Westbend Co.
West Bend, WI 53095
414/334-6922

Westinghouse
Gateway Center
Westinghouse Bldg.
Pittsburg, PA 15222
412/255-3800

Whirlpool
Administrative Center
Benton Harbor, MI 49022
616/926-5000